# KEMETAN CALENDAR

# AND ZODIAC
## FIRST EDITION

**TARÍK KARENGA**

AMENISM, INC.

UNION CITY, CALIFORNIA

Vivian Azad, *thess em hotep* (rise up in peace).

# TABLE OF CONTENTS

# LIST OF ILLUSTRATIONS

## TABLES

## PLATES

# THE REVOCATION OF THE EDICTS OF THEODOSIUS AND JUSTINIAN

Citizens of Kemet⌐🦅̥, in the year 50941 of our calendar and following a complex series of historical events that eventually led to the fall of our civilization, the Roman Emperor Theodosius issued an edict which ordered the closing of Kemetan temples; however, it was not until almost a century and a half later that the last Kemetan temples on the island of Philae were closed, following a second edict issued by Emperor Justinian.[1] Still, further injury to our people was sustained due to an insidious cultural shift that was brought about by the adoption of Christianity and by our subsequent conversion to the religion of Islam, but as a whole, we as Africans have had no other greater immoral or atrocious injury inflicted upon us than that of the Holocaust of Enslavement, which claimed an estimated 50 to 100 million lives through ". . . mass murder, war, the forcible transfer of populations, and the brutal rigors of the Middle Passage and of enslavement as well as the attendant dehumanization and cultural destruction."[2] Notwithstanding, we have endured through it all—even to the extent that we have now begun to restore ourselves and to re-project our own priorities.

For the record, we are descended from the ancient Kemetans, ". . . the exclusive inventors of the calendar . . ." and therefore we are asserting our right to return the Kemetan calendar to its original configuration from its reconfigured form dubbed the Gregorian calendar, which ". . . regulates our life today," but which also continues to disadvantage us by undermining our religion, devaluing our culture and normalizing irrelevancy in the experiences of our life.[3] To that end, the edicts of Theodosius and Justinian are hereby revoked and all Kemetan temples are ordered reopened forthwith as the first initial steps toward repairing the injuries of the past in lieu of becoming dependent upon the identified offend-

---

1. Tarík Karenga, *The Pharaohs' 5 Laws of Success*, First Edition, (Union City: Amenism, Inc., 2022), 25, 57-58. The Reemergent Kingdom of Kemet began in the year 52580 Z.T.E. (Kemetan Calendar) or 2020 C.E. (Gregorian calendar). *Ibid.*, 55. *See* also George G. M. James, *Stolen Legacy*, (Trenton: African World Press, 1992), 37, 39. *See* also Table 7.

2. George G. M. James, *Stolen Legacy*, (Trenton: African World Press, 1992), 37-38. *See* also James P. Allen, *Middle Egyptian: An Introduction to the Language and Culture of Hieroglyphs*, (New York: Cambridge University Press, 2001), 11. *See* also Maulana Karenga, *Introduction to Black Studies*, Second Edition, (Los Angeles: University of Sankore Press, 1993), 115.

3. Tarík Karenga, *The Pharaohs' 5 Laws of Success*, First Edition, (Union City: Amenism, Inc., 2022), 57-59. *See* also the term *black*, in Tarík Karenga, *Review of the Kemetan Mystery System*, First Edition, (Union City: Amenism, Inc., in press). *See* also Cheikh Anta Diop, *Civilization or Barbarism: An Authentic Anthropology*, (Brooklyn: Lawrence Hill Books, 1991), 279. *See* also Rekhety Wimby Jones, "The Calendar Project," in *African World History Project: The Preliminary Challenge*, eds. Jacob H. Carruthers and Leon C. Harris, (Los Angeles: Association for the Study of Classical African Civilizations, 1997), 105.

ers for reparations.[4]  That is to say, reparations is not what others do for us on their own and in isolation, but rather, reparations is what we do for one another together, and as a community.[5]

—Tarík Karenga

*Given in the month of Paen Khonsu, in the year 52582, and in the third year of our reign.*

---

4. The opening of the "temple of the spirit" precedes the opening of the "temple of the world." *See* the terms *Kemet, Kingdom of God on Earth* and *Kingdom of Heaven*, in Tarík Karenga, *Review of the Kemetan Mystery System*, First Edition, (Union City: Amenism, Inc., in press).

5. This teaching pertaining to reparations comes down to us from Pharaoh Queen Hatshepsut who said that she restored what had been ruined and raised up what had been damaged by the foreign invaders called Hyksos. *See* Maulana Karenga, *Maat: The Moral Ideal in Ancient Egypt*, (Los Angeles: University of Sankore Press, 2006), 80, 398.

# CHAPTER ONE

# THE CALENDAR

Returning the calendar to its original configuration begins by recognizing that ours is a tri-narrative solar calendar that speaks to harmonizing the relationship between God, humankind and nature, as viewed through the life cycles of the soul, its human host and the environment in four well-defined stages of life here presented.[1]

**Stage 1:** The emergence of the soul and its passage from the realm of spirit into the physical realm. The religion of Amenism teaches that God Amen (ah-**MEN**) in his name of Ra (**RAH**) is **spirit** in its phase of **soul** symbolically represented as the Sun, that he is self-created, and that he emerged from nonexistence or nothing–Ñun (**NYOON**).[2] In a hymn of praise, a Kemetan scribe identifies God with Ñun in the following manner:

*"He cannot be sculptured in stone in figures whereon is placed the White Crown.*

*He cannot be seen. Service cannot be rendered to him. Gifts cannot be presented*

---

1. A tri-narrative is defined as three separate accounts of connected events that reveal one underlying truth viewed from three different perspectives. According to Amenism the Kemetan calendar, which is a tri-narrative and a solar calendar, was also the formal calendar for the highly formalistic civilization of ancient Kemet. *See* Cheikh Anta Diop, *The African Origin of Civilization: Myth or Reality*, (Chicago: Lawrence Hill Books, 1974), 91, Note 16.

2. Serge Sauneron and Jean Yoyotte, "La Naissance Du Monde Selon L'Egypte Ancienne," in *Sources Orientales I: La Naissance Du Monde*, eds. Anne-Marie Esnoul, Paul Garelli, Yves Hervouet, Marcel Leibovici, Serge Sauneron and Jean Yoyotte, (Paris: Editions Du Seuil, 1959), 22-23. *See* also E. A. Wallis Budge, *The Book of the Dead: The Papyrus of Ani in the British Museum*, (London: Kegan Paul, Trench, Trubner & Co., 1895), xcix, cvii. *See* also Tarík Karenga, *The Pharaohs' 5 Laws of Success*, First Edition, (Union City: Amenism, Inc., 2022), 11. Note: In what present-day Amenists recognize as Kemet's Reemergent Kingdom, Ō is transliterated *ny* and spelled ny and ñ (*i.e.*, the letter -n- with a tilde overhead; Wolof form), and is pronounced "ny" as in the Wolof language of the West African country of Senegal. The genetic relationship of modern African languages such as Wolof to the ancient Kemetan language has been well documented; furthermore, scholar and author Rekhety Wimby states: ". . . the languages of Africa all derive, by evolutionary processes, from an original parent, to which I give the name, suggested by C. A. Diop in *Parente genetique*, Paleo-African." Rekhety Wimby, "The Unity of African Languages," in *Kemet and the African Worldview*, eds. Maulana Karenga and Jacob Carruthers, (Los Angeles: University of Sankore Press, 1986), 151-166. Cheikh Anta Diop, *The Cultural Unity of Black Africa*, (London: Karnak House, 1989), 168-169. Ñu vase transliterations: *nyu* and *nyw*, spelled ñu and pronounced "nyoo." *See* E. A. Wallis Budge, *An Egyptian Hieroglyphic Dictionary: In Two Volumes*, Volume I, (London: John Murray, 1920), 349a-b. Alan Gardiner, *Egyptian Grammar: Being an Introduction to the Study of Hieroglyphs*, Third Edition, Revised, (Oxford: Griffith Institute, 1994), 530, 573a. The term "Amenism" herein refers to Amenism the religion according to the Reemergent Kingdom, which works interdependently with and is an integral part of the Kemetan Mystery System, so for all intents and purposes the religion and the Mystery System are virtually one and the same. George G. M. James, *Stolen Legacy*, (Trenton: African World Press, 1992), 1ff. *See* also Tarík Karenga, *Review of the Kemetan Mystery System*, First Edition, (Union City: Amenism, Inc., in press).

*to him.  He is not to be approached in the sanctuaries.  Where he is is not known.*

*He is not to be found in inscribed shrines.  No habitation can contain him.*

*There is none who acteth as guide to his heart.*"[3]

Notwithstanding, this nothingness was envisaged as a vast, abysmal and primordial ocean from which the Sun (*i.e.*, soul or Ra) first emerged.[4]  Furthermore, it is taught that Osir, the first person of the Holy Trinity that came down to earth from heaven, is the soul of Ra and that these seemingly two different Gods are actually one and the same, for as we read in the Litany of Ra:

"*. . . the birth of [[Osir]] is the birth of Ra in the Ament, and reciprocally;*

*the birth of [[Osir]] in the heavens is the birth of the soul of Ra in the heavens,*

*and reciprocally; the life of [[Osir]] is the life of Ra, and reciprocally;*

*the development of his body is the development of Ra's body.*"[5]

The two births mentioned above are the first two markers employed when calibrating the calendar, whereby the birth of Osir is, from a different perspective, the emergence of the soul or the birth of Ra in "Amenta" (*i.e.*, heaven located in the realm of spirit) and corresponds to the *first* of five officially named "days over the year" on which the birthdays of Osir, Heru-ur (*i.e.*, Heru as an Elder), Seth, Iset and Nebt-Het respectively are celebrated just before the commencement of the New Year consisting ". . . of twelve months, each containing thirty days (divided into three ten-day weeks), in all **360 days**" plus five intercalary days; hence, the "days over the year" constituting the **calendrical five-day period** that corresponds to the five-day period of the summer solstice when the Sun appears to stand still or rise from the same spot for approximately five days in a row, having apparently reached ". . . its maximum distance north . . . of the celestial equator" (*see* Tables 1 and 2).[6]

3. E. A. Wallis Budge, Tutankhamen: *Amenism, Atenism and Egyptian Monotheism*, (London: Martin Hopkinson, 1923), 143.

4. Serge Sauneron and Jean Yoyotte, "La Naissance Du Monde Selon L'Egypte Ancienne," in *Sources Orientales I: La Naissance Du Monde*, eds. Anne-Marie Esnoul, Paul Garelli, Yves Hervouet, Marcel Leibovici, Serge Sauneron and Jean Yoyotte, (Paris: Editions Du Seuil, 1959), 22-23. *See* also E. A. Wallis Budge, *The Book of the Dead: The Papyrus of Ani in the British Museum*, (London: Kegan Paul, Trench, Trubner & Co., 1895), xcix, cvii. *See* also Tarík Karenga, *The Pharaohs' 5 Laws of Success*, First Edition, (Union City: Amenism, Inc., 2022), 76 note 15.

5. Edouard Naville, "The Litany of Ra," in *Records of the Past*, Volume VIII, Egyptian Texts, ed. Samuel Birch, (London: Samuel Bagster and Sons, 1874), 120. Italics mine. [[ ]] Double brackets indicate word or term substitution made by the author. Here, the spelling of the name "Osir," which refers to the first person of God Ra, is consistent with the teachings of Amenism and has therefore been substituted for the name "Osiris," which is Greek. *See* also Tarík Karenga, *The Pharaohs' 5 Laws of Success*, First Edition, (Union City: Amenism, Inc., 2022), 15.

6. Edouard Naville, "The Litany of Ra," in *Records of the Past*, Volume VIII, Egyptian Texts, ed. Samuel Birch, (London: Samuel Bagster and Sons, 1874), 105, 120. Mine in parentheses. E. A. Wallis Budge, *The Mummy: A Handbook of Egyptian Funerary Archaeology*, Second Edition, Revised & Greatly Enlarged, (London: Cambridge University Press, 1925), 479. Mine in parentheses. *See* also "solstice" in Webster's New World Dictionary & Thesaurus, Version 2.0, Build #25,

## Table 1: Months and Seasons of the Year

| Months and Seasons[7] | Medu Netur | Meaning[8] | Coptic[9] |
|---|---|---|---|
| *Shemu: Season of Inundation (Summer)* [10] | | | |
| 1. Mesut Ra  (**MAY-SOOT  RAH**) | [hieroglyphs] [11] | Birth of Ra [New Year] | Mesore |

Accent Software International, Macmillan Publishers, 1998. *See* also Tyler Nordgren, *Stars Above, Earth Below: A Guide to Astronomy in the National Parks*, (Chichester: Praxis Publishing Ltd., 2010), 277-278. That the day of the summer solstice is the longest day of the year, the period of the summer solstice is two days longer than that of the winter solstice. According to the teachings of the religion of Amenism. Note: Here, the Sun (soul) passes from the zodiacal sign Aquarius to that of Capricorn; hence the "He-Goat Fish" leaping out of the water and onto dry land. For the ten-day week in hieroglyphs, *see* E. A. Wallis Budge, *An Egyptian Hieroglyphic Dictionary: In Two Volumes*, Volume I, (London: John Murray, 1920), 53b, 331a. *See* the term *heaven*, in Tarík Karenga, *Review of the Kemetan Mystery System*, First Edition, (Union City: Amenism, Inc., in press).

7. Juan Antonio Belmonte, "The Egyptian Calendar: Keeping Ma'at on Earth," in *In Search of Cosmic Order: Selected Essays on Egyptian Archaeoastronomy*, eds. Juan Antonio Belmonte and Mosalam Shaltout, (Cairo: Supreme Council of Antiquities, 2009), 99. *See* also Raymond Weill, *Etudes D'Egyptologie: Bases, Methodes et Resultats de la Chronologie Egyptienne*, (Paris: Paul Geuthner, 1926), 113. A few modifications have been made for the Reemergent Kingdom and are to be found in the notes for this table under the column heading "Meaning."

8. Juan Antonio Belmonte, "The Egyptian Calendar: Keeping Ma'at on Earth," in *In Search of Cosmic Order: Selected Essays on Egyptian Archaeoastronomy*, eds. Juan Antonio Belmonte and Mosalam Shaltout, (Cairo: Supreme Council of Antiquities, 2009), 99. In the Reemergent Kingdom "Oup Renpet," meaning the "Opening of the Year" is the **calendrical five-day period** comprising the five "days over the year" for observing the birthdays of Osir, Heru-ur, Seth, Iset and Nebt-Het respectively, while the actual first month of the year, according to Egyptologist Alan Gardiner, is Mesut Ra, meaning the "birth of Ra." *See* E. A. Wallis Budge, *An Egyptian Hieroglyphic Dictionary: In Two Volumes*, Volume I, (London: John Murray, 1920), cxiii, 161b. *Oup* (**OHP**) means "open" or "opening," whereas *a oup* (ah-**OHP**) means "to open." *Ibid.*, 33b. *Renpet* means "year;" the related word *renpi* means "to be young." *Ibid.*, 427ab. E. A. Wallis Budge, *First Steps in Egyptian: A Book for Beginners*, (London: Kegan Paul, Trench, Trubner & Co., Ltd., 1895), 35. Note: "Renpet," pronounced (**REN**-pet). Also, *Oupur* (ohp-**OOR**) means "opener." *Ibid.*, 252. *See* also Alan H. Gardiner, "Mesore as First Month of the Egyptian Year," in *Zeitschrift Fur Agyptische Sprache Und Altertumskunde*, Volume 43, eds. A. Erman and G. Steindorff, (Leipzig: J. C. Hinrichs'sche Buchhandlung, 1906), 136-144. For the month "Ka Hera Ka" *see ibid.*, 139. [ ] Brackets indicate interpolation to clarify the meaning. For example, the word for "face" *i.e.*, "hera," when preceded by the word "en" literally means on the face of; hence, upon. *See* E. A. Wallis Budge, *The Gods of the Egyptians: Or, Studies in Egyptian Mythology*, Volume I, (London: Methuen & Company, 1904), 466. *See* also E. A. Wallis Budge, *An Egyptian Hieroglyphic Dictionary: In Two Volumes*, Volume I, (London: John Murray, 1920), 339a, 492b, 493a. For the month "Tybi" *see* Jaroslav Cerny, "The Origin of the Name of the Month Tybi," in *Annales Du Service Des Antiquites De L'Egypte*, Tome XLIII, (Cairo: Imprimerie De L'Institut Francais D'Archeologie Orientale, 1943), 179. For the month "Makhiar" *see* E. A. Wallis Budge, *The Gods of the Egyptians: Or, Studies in Egyptian Mythology*, Volume II, (London: Methuen & Company, 1904), 293 (note 4). For the month "Ap Ap," harvests would have been assessed beginning in the first two months of the season of Pert while the harvest taxes would have been collected at the end of the year in the month of Ap Ap to which was attached a sarcastic saying concerning the peasant: "His reckoning lasts until eternity." *See* Hermann Kees, *Ancient Egypt: A Cultural Topography*, (London: Faber and Faber, 1961), 58-59. *See* also E. A. Wallis Budge, *An Egyptian Hieroglyphic Dictionary: In Two Volumes*, Volume I, (London: John Murray, 1920), 41a-b.

9. E. A. Wallis Budge, *The Book of Kings*, Volume I, Dynasties I-XIX, (London: Kegan Paul, Trench, Trubner & Co., Ltd., 1908), XLIV.

10. E. A. Wallis Budge, *An Egyptian Hieroglyphic Dictionary: In Two Volumes*, Volume II, (London: John Murray, 1920), 740a. E. A. Wallis Budge, *Facsimiles of Egyptian Hieratic Papyri in the British Museum*, Series 1, (London: Oxford University Press, 1910), xvi.

11. Alan H. Gardiner, "Mesore as First Month of the Egyptian Year," in *Zeitschrift Fur Agyptische Sprache Und*

| 2. Tekhi   (TEK-ee) | | (Month of) Tekhi | Thoth |
|---|---|---|---|
| 3. Paen Aopet   (PAH-en OH-pet) | | This (month of) Aopet | Paophi |
| 4. Het-Heru   (HET hay-ROO) | | (Month of) Het-Heru | Athyr |

*Akhet: Season of Sowing (Winter)* [15]

| 5. Ka Hera Ka   (KA HAIR-uh KA) | | Ka Upon Ka | Khoiak |
|---|---|---|---|
| 6. Ta Aobyti   (TAH oh-BIT-ee) | | (Month of) The Offering | Tybi |
| 7. Makhiar   (mah-kee-AR) | | (Month of) Makhiar | Mekhir |
| 8. Paen Amenhotep (PAH-en AMEN-ho-TEP) | | This (month of) Amenhotep | Phamenoth |

*Altertumskunde*, Volume 43, eds. A. Erman and G. Steindorff, (Leipzig: J. C. Hinrichs'sche Buchhandlung, 1906), 142. cf. E. A. Wallis Budge, *An Egyptian Hieroglyphic Dictionary: In Two Volumes*, Volume I, (London: John Murray, 1920), 321b.

12. Raymond Weill, *Etudes D'Egyptologie: Bases, Methodes et Resultats de la Chronologie Egyptienne*, (Paris: Paul Geuthner, 1926), 113. *See* also E. A. Wallis Budge, *An Egyptian Hieroglyphic Dictionary: In Two Volumes*, Volume II, (London: John Murray, 1920), 842b.

13. E. A. Wallis Budge, *An Egyptian Hieroglyphic Dictionary: In Two Volumes*, Volume I, (London: John Murray, 1920), 236a-b. "PAH-en" is the pronunciation for p + n. Adolf Erman, "Monatsnamen aus dem neuen Reich," in *Zeitschrift Fur Agyptische Sprache Und Altertumskunde*, Volume 39, eds. A. Erman and G. Steindorff, (Leipzig: J. C. Hinrichs'sche Buchhandlung, 1901), 130. Adolf Erman and Hermann Grapow, *Worterbuch Der* Aegyptischen Sprache, Volume 1, (Berlin: Akademie -Verlag, 1971), 492.

14. Raymond Weill, *Etudes D'Egyptologie: Bases, Methodes et Resultats de la Chronologie Egyptienne*, (Paris: Paul Geuthner, 1926), 113. Alan Gardiner, *Egyptian Grammar: Being an Introduction to the Study of Hieroglyphs*, Third Edition, Revised, (Oxford: Griffith Institute, 1994), 494.

15. E. A. Wallis Budge, *An Egyptian Hieroglyphic Dictionary: In Two Volumes*, Volume I, (London: John Murray, 1920), 8b. E. A. Wallis Budge, *Facsimiles of Egyptian Hieratic Papyri in the British Museum*, Series 1, (London: Oxford University Press, 1910), xvi.

16. Raymond Weill, *Etudes D'Egyptologie: Bases, Methodes et Resultats de la Chronologie Egyptienne*, (Paris: Paul Geuthner, 1926), 113. [ ] Brackets indicate interpolation to clarify the meaning. *See* also E. A. Wallis Budge, *An Egyptian Hieroglyphic Dictionary: In Two Volumes*, Volume I, (London: John Murray, 1920), 339a.

17. E. A. Wallis Budge, *An Egyptian Hieroglyphic Dictionary: In Two Volumes*, Volume I, (London: John Murray, 1920), 117a. E. A. Wallis Budge, *An Egyptian Hieroglyphic Dictionary: In Two Volumes*, Volume II, (London: John Murray, 1920), 815a. Jaroslav Cerny, "The Origin of the Name of the Month Tybi," in *Annales Du Service Des Antiquites De L'Egypte*, Tome XLIII, (Cairo: Imprimerie De L'Institut Francais D'Archeologie Orientale, 1943), 179.

18. E. A. Wallis Budge, *The Gods of the Egyptians: Or, Studies in Egyptian Mythology*, Volume II, (London: Methuen & Company, 1904), 293 (note 4). *See* also E. A. Wallis Budge, *An Egyptian Hieroglyphic Dictionary: In Two Volumes*, Volume I, (London: John Murray, 1920), 286a.

19. E. A. Wallis Budge, *An Egyptian Hieroglyphic Dictionary: In Two Volumes*, Volume I, (London: John Murray, 1920), 236a-b. "PAH-en" is the pronunciation for p + n. Adolf Erman, "Monatsnamen aus dem neuen Reich," in *Zeitschrift Fur Agyptische Sprache Und Altertumskunde*, Volume 39, eds. A. Erman and G. Steindorff, (Leipzig: J. C. Hinrichs'sche Buchhandlung, 1901), 130. Adolf Erman and Hermann Grapow, *Worterbuch Der* Aegyptischen Sprache, Volume 1, (Berlin:

 *Pert: Season of Growing and Harvesting (Spring)* [20]

| | | | | |
|---|---|---|---|---|
| 9. Paen Renñutet | (**PAH**-en ren-**NYOO**-tet) |  [21] | This (month of ) Renñutet | Pharmuthi |
| 10. Paen Khonsu | (**PAH**-en **COAN**-soo) |  [22] | This (month of ) Khonsu | Pakhon |
| 11. Paen Aynit | (**PAH**-en **AI**-neet) |  [23] | This (month of) the Valley | Payni |
| 12. Ap Ap | (**AHP AHP**) | 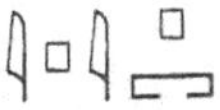 [24] | Reckon! Reckon! [Month of *Harvest Tax* Collection] | Epiphi |
| Oup Renpet | (**OHP REN**-pet) |  [25] | Opening of the Year [*Calendrical Five-Day Period*] | - |

*Source:* Amenism. *The names of the months in what modern Amenists recognize as Kemet's Reemergent Kingdom*

Akademie -Verlag, 1971), 492.

20. E. A. Wallis Budge, *An Egyptian Hieroglyphic Dictionary: In Two Volumes*, Volume I, (London: John Murray, 1920), 242b. E. A. Wallis Budge, *Facsimiles of Egyptian Hieratic Papyri in the British Museum*, Series 1, (London: Oxford University Press, 1910), xvi.

21. E. A. Wallis Budge, *An Egyptian Hieroglyphic Dictionary: In Two Volumes*, Volume I, (London: John Murray, 1920), 236a, 427a. "**PAH**-en" is the pronunciation for p + n. Adolf Erman, "Monatsnamen aus dem neuen Reich," in *Zeitschrift Fur Agyptische Sprache Und Altertumskunde*, Volume 39, eds. A. Erman and G. Steindorff, (Leipzig: J. C. Hinrichs'sche Buchhandlung, 1901), 130. Adolf Erman and Hermann Grapow, *Worterbuch Der* Aegyptischen Sprache, Volume 1, (Berlin: Akademie -Verlag, 1971), 492.

22. E. A. Wallis Budge, *An Egyptian Hieroglyphic Dictionary: In Two Volumes*, Volume I, (London: John Murray, 1920), 236a, 553a. "**PAH**-en" is the pronunciation for p + n. Adolf Erman, "Monatsnamen aus dem neuen Reich," in *Zeitschrift Fur Agyptische Sprache Und Altertumskunde*, Volume 39, eds. A. Erman and G. Steindorff, (Leipzig: J. C. Hinrichs'sche Buchhandlung, 1901), 130. Adolf Erman and Hermann Grapow, *Worterbuch D*er Aegyptischen Sprache, Volume 1, (Berlin: Akademie -Verlag, 1971), 492.

23. E. A. Wallis Budge, *An Egyptian Hieroglyphic Dictionary: In Two Volumes*, Volume I, (London: John Murray, 1920), 58a, 236a-b. *See* also Gunther Roeder, *Short Egyptian Grammar*, (New Haven: Yale University Press, 1920), 57. "**PAH**-en" is the pronunciation for p + n. Adolf Erman, "Monatsnamen aus dem neuen Reich," in *Zeitschrift Fur Agyptische Sprache Und Altertumskunde*, Volume 39, eds. A. Erman and G. Steindorff, (Leipzig: J. C. Hinrichs'sche Buchhandlung, 1901), 130. Adolf Erman and Hermann Grapow, *Worterbuc*h Der Aegyptischen Sprache, Volume 1, (Berlin: Akademie -Verlag, 1971), 492.

24. E. A. Wallis Budge, *An Egyptian Hieroglyphic Dictionary: In Two Volumes*, Volume I, (London: John Murray, 1920), 41b.

25. E. A. Wallis Budge, *An Egyptian Hieroglyphic Dictionary: In Two Volumes*, Volume I, (London: John Murray, 1920), cxiii, 161b. *Oup* (**OHP**) means "open" or "opening," whereas *a oup* (ah-**OHP**) means "to open." *Ibid.*, 33b. *Renpet* means "year;" the related word *renpi* means "to be young." *Ibid.*, 427ab. E. A. Wallis Budge, *First Steps in Egyptian: A Book for Beginners*, (London: Kegan Paul, Trench, Trubner & Co., Ltd., 1895), 35. Note: "Renpet," pronounced (**REN**-pet). Also, *Oupur* (ohp-**OOR**) means "opener." *Ibid.*, 252. *See* also Adolf Erman and Hermann Grapow, *Worterbuch Der* Aegyptischen Sprache, Volume 1, (Berlin: Akademie -Verlag, 1971), 300.

**Table 2: Days of the Week**

| Days of the Week[26] | Medu Netur | Contextual Meaning | Colloquial |
|---|---|---|---|
| 1.  Ra   (**RAH**) | [27] | (Day of) Ra | Day-Ra |
| 2.  Khnum   (kuh-**NOOM**) | [28] | (Day of) Khnum | Day-Khnum |
| 3.  Bast   (**BAHST**) | [29] | (Day of) Bast | Day-Bast |
| 4.  Sobek   (**SO**-bek) | [30] | (Day of) Sobek | Day-Sobek |
| 5.  Tauret   (taow-**RET**) | [31] | (Day of) Tauret | Day-Tauret |
| 6.  Mut   (**MOOT**) | [32] | (Day of) Mut | Day-Mut |
| 7.  Amen   (ah-**MEN**) | [33] | (Day of) Amen | Day-Amen |
| 8.  Sekhmet   (**SEKH**-met) | [34] | (Day of) Sekhmet | Day-Sekhmet |

26. Dio Cassius (Roman statesman and historian) once said, "The custom, however, of referring the days (of the week) to the seven stars called planets was instituted by the Egyptians;" that is to say, a compact modified version of the Kemetan calendar contained a seven-day week, *e.g.*, "Saturn, Jupiter, Mars, Sun, Venus, Mercury, Moon." E. H. Warmington, *Dio's Roman History*, In Nine Volumes, III, (Cambridge: Harvard University Press, 1969), 129, 131. Mine in parentheses. *See* also James Johnston, "Traces of a Sabbath in Heathen Lands," in *The Catholic Presbyterian*, Volume V, (New York: A. D. F. Randolph & Co., 1881), 204-205. Note: Dio Cassius makes no mention of the Kemetan ten-day week; notwithstanding, it is here presented according to the teachings of Amenism in the Reemergent Kingdom. The day of Ra, who is symbolically represented as the Sun, is the first day of the week; *see* "Stage 1" above. The tenth day of the week is the day of Hapi, meaning the Nile River, which symbolically represents Ñun from which Ra first emerged and then established the first day, and into which, according to Amenist Scripture, everything created by God will return in the end. Walter Beyerlin, ed., *Near Eastern Religious Texts Relating to the Old Testament*, (Philadelphia: The Westminster Press, 1978), 12. E. A. Wallis Budge, Tutankhamen: *Amenism, Atenism and Egyptian Monotheism*, (London: Martin Hopkinson, 1923), 143. *See* also "Stage 1" above.

27. E. A. Wallis Budge, *An Egyptian Hieroglyphic Dictionary: In Two Volumes*, Volume I, (London: John Murray, 1920), 418a. Felix Guirand, *Larousse Encyclopedia of Mythology*, (New York: Prometheus Press, 1960), 12-13.

28. E. A. Wallis Budge, *An Egyptian Hieroglyphic Dictionary: In Two Volumes*, Volume I, (London: John Murray, 1920), 578a. Felix Guirand, *Larousse Encyclopedia of Mythology*, (New York: Prometheus Press, 1960), 37.

29. E. A. Wallis Budge, *An Egyptian Hieroglyphic Dictionary: In Two Volumes*, Volume I, (London: John Murray, 1920), 205a, b. Felix Guirand, *Larousse Encyclopedia of Mythology*, (New York: Prometheus Press, 1960), 36.

30. E. A. Wallis Budge, *An Egyptian Hieroglyphic Dictionary: In Two Volumes*, Volume II, (London: John Murray, 1920), 660a. Felix Guirand, *Larousse Encyclopedia of Mythology*, (New York: Prometheus Press, 1960), 34-35.

31. E. A. Wallis Budge, *An Egyptian Hieroglyphic Dictionary: In Two Volumes*, Volume II, (London: John Murray, 1920), 819b. Felix Guirand, *Larousse Encyclopedia of Mythology*, (New York: Prometheus Press, 1960), 38, 40.

32. E. A. Wallis Budge, *An Egyptian Hieroglyphic Dictionary: In Two Volumes*, Volume I, (London: John Murray, 1920), 295a. Felix Guirand, *Larousse Encyclopedia of Mythology*, (New York: Prometheus Press, 1960), 32, 34.

33. E. A. Wallis Budge, *An Egyptian Hieroglyphic Dictionary: In Two Volumes*, Volume I, (London: John Murray, 1920), 51b. Felix Guirand, *Larousse Encyclopedia of Mythology*, (New York: Prometheus Press, 1960), 30-32.

34. E. A. Wallis Budge, *An Egyptian Hieroglyphic Dictionary: In Two Volumes*, Volume II, (London: John Murray, 1920), 691b. Felix Guirand, *Larousse Encyclopedia of Mythology*, (New York: Prometheus Press, 1960), 35-36.

| | | | | |
|---|---|---|---|---|
| 9. Ptah | (p-**TAH**) | [hieroglyphs] 35 | (Day of) Ptah | Day-Ptah |
| 10. Hapi | (**HAH**-pee) | [hieroglyphs] 36 | (Day of) Hapi | Day-Hapi |

*Source:* Amenism. *The names of the days of the week in the Reemergent Kingdom*

In the Northern Hemisphere where ancient Kemet was situated geographically, ". . . the longest day of the year . . ." is called the <u>day</u> of the summer solstice; however, the **calendrical five-day period** comprising the five "days over the year" and that corresponds to the five-day period of the summer solstice is called Oup Renpet (**OHP REN**-pet), meaning the "Opening of the Year" (*see* Table 3).[37] Now, around the same time as the five-day summer solstice period, the annual rains in the highlands of Ethiopia (new name for Abyssinia) begin falling across the countryside ". . . from June until early October," and it was these very rains that caused the annual inundation or flooding of the River Nile, whose anticipated rise coincided with the birthday of Osir, symbolizing his emergence from Ñun.[38]

**Table 3:**[39]           **Oup Renpet and the Five-Day Summer Solstice Period**

| Date | Birthday | Pronunciation | Description | Gregorian |
|---|---|---|---|---|
| Oup Renpet 1 | Osir | (oh-**SEER**) | * *First day of the five-day summer solstice period.* The Nile River begins to rise.<br><br>"(T)he birth of Osir" in Amenta.[40] | June 20 |

35. E. A. Wallis Budge, *An Egyptian Hieroglyphic Dictionary: In Two Volumes*, Volume I, (London: John Murray, 1920), 254b. Felix Guirand, *Larousse Encyclopedia of Mythology*, (New York: Prometheus Press, 1960), 35.

36. E. A. Wallis Budge, *An Egyptian Hieroglyphic Dictionary: In Two Volumes*, Volume I, (London: John Murray, 1920), 467a, b. Felix Guirand, *Larousse Encyclopedia of Mythology*, (New York: Prometheus Press, 1960), 37-38.

37. Eric Chaisson and Steve McMillan, *Astronomy: A Beginner's Guide to the Universe*, Fifth Edition, (Upper Saddle River: Pearson Prentice Hall, 2007), 10. *See* also, E. A. Wallis Budge, *An Egyptian Hieroglyphic Dictionary: In Two Volumes*, Volume I, (London: John Murray, 1920), 161b. E. A. Wallis Budge, *First Steps in Egyptian: A Book for Beginners*, (London: Kegan Paul, Trench, Trubner & Co., Ltd., 1895), 35. *See* also Adolf Erman and Hermann Grapow, *Worterbuch Der Aegyptischen Sprache*, Volume 1, (Berlin: Akademie -Verlag, 1971), 300.

38. Philip Briggs, *Ethiopia*, Sixth Edition, (Guilford: The Globe Pequot Press Inc., 2012), 75. *See* also "Abyssinia" in Webster's New World Dictionary & Thesaurus, Version 2.0, Build #25, Accent Software International, Macmillan Publishers, 1998. "After the beginning of the rainy season in Ethiopia the river (Nile) started to rise early in June." Rushdi Said, *The River Nile: Geology, Hydrology and Utilization*, (Tarrytown: Pergamon Press, 1993), 21, 96-97. Mine in parentheses. For the table showing the rise of the Nile on June 20th (Gregorian), *see Ibid.*, 97. *See* also W. Marsham Adams, *Book of the Master: Or the Egyptian Doctrine of the Light Born of the Virgin Mother*, (New York: G. P. Putnam's Sons, 1898), 62. That Karl Baedeker reports the date of June 21st (Gregorian) as the day on which the Nile begins to rise, the discrepancy of one day is of no real consequence. *See* Karl Baedeker, *Egypt: Handbook for Travellers*, Fifth Edition, (New York: Charles Scribner's Sons, 1902), lxxvii.

39. For sources of spellings of names and of pronunciations *see* Tarík Karenga, *The Pharaohs' 5 Laws of Success*, First Edition, (Union City: Amenism, Inc., 2022), 15.

40. *See* above.

| Oup Renpet 2 | Heru-ur | (hay-**ROO-OOR**) *i.e.*, Heru (as an Elder) | * *Second day of the five-day summer solstice period **falls on the <u>day</u> of the summer solstice.*** | June 21 |
|---|---|---|---|---|
| Oup Renpet 3 | Seth | (Seth) | * *Third day of the five-day summer solstice period.*  **Also on this day began ". . . the jurisdiction of the Great Divine Ennead" for ending the confusion created by Seth.**[41] | June 22 |
| Oup Renpet 4 | Iset | (ee-**SET**) | * *Fourth day of the five-day summer solstice period.* | June 23 |
| Oup Renpet 5 | Nebt-Het | (nebt-**HET**) | * *Fifth day of the five-day summer solstice period.* | June 24 |

"(T)he birth of Osir in the heavens" (*i.e.*, the sky in the physical realm) is in reference to the Amenist teaching that Osir, ". . . at whose entrance into the world a voice was heard, saying, 'the lord of all the earth is born,'" came down to earth from heaven, and corresponds to the astronomical event in which the Sun, having appeared to stand still or rise from the same spot for approximately five days in a row during the period of the summer solstice and at its apparent maximum distance north of the celestial equator, reverses its movement and **begins to *visibly* rise increasingly southward**, officially observed on the first day of the month of Mesut Ra (**MAY-SOOT RAH**), meaning the "birth of Ra" (*i.e.*, the birth of the Sun and the entrance of the soul into the world) or on June 25th (Gregorian), which is also the first day of the season of Shemu (she-**MOO**) *i.e.*, the season of inundation, and **New Year's Day** (*see* Plate 1).[42]

---

41. Maulana Karenga, *Maat: The Moral Ideal in Ancient Egypt*, (Los Angeles: University of Sankore Press, 2006), 206.

42. Edouard Naville, "The Litany of Ra," in *Records of the Past*, Volume VIII, Egyptian Texts, ed. Samuel Birch, (London: Samuel Bagster and Sons, 1874), 120. Mine in parentheses. E. A. Wallis Budge, *The Gods of the Egyptians: Or, Studies in Egyptian Mythology*, Volume II, (London: Methuen & Company, 1904), 186. Tarík Karenga, *The Pharaohs' 5 Laws of Success*, First Edition, (Union City: Amenism, Inc., 2022), 54-55. *See* also "solstice" in Webster's New World Dictionary & Thesaurus, Version 2.0, Build #25, Accent Software International, Macmillan Publishers, 1998. *See* also Tyler Nordgren, *Stars Above, Earth Below: A Guide to Astronomy in the National Parks*, (Chichester: Praxis Publishing Ltd., 2010), 277-278. According to Egyptologist Alan Gardiner, the first month of the year was originally Mesut Ra; however, the month-names ". . . have in the course of ages receded one place backwards." That the ancient Kemetans intentionally changed most of the month-names during the New Kingdom, it is probable that if there was a shifting of the month-names "one place backwards" then it too may have been intentional; in any case, such a shift certainly could cause the calendar to fall out of sync with the seasons, notwithstanding according to Amenism, leap year rules for the calendar were already being employed. *See* James P. Allen, *Middle Egyptian: An Introduction to the Language and Culture of Hieroglyphs*, (New York: Cambridge University Press, 2001), 108. *See* also Alan H. Gardiner, "Mesore as First Month of the Egyptian Year," in *Zeitschrift Fur Agyptische Sprache Und Altertumskunde*, Volume 43, eds. A. Erman and G. Steindorff, (Leipzig: J. C. Hinrichs'sche Buchhandlung, 1906), 140, 142. Additionally, it was on the first day of Mesut Ra that Osir entered the world, hence, the birth of Ra. For season-names *see* E. A. Wallis Budge, *Facsimiles of Egyptian Hieratic Papyri in the British Museum*, Series 1, (London: Oxford University Press, 1910), xvi. *See* also E. A. Wallis Budge, *An Egyptian Hieroglyphic Dictionary: In Two*

Knowledge of the solstices, then, was factored into synchronizing the calendar with the seasons and harmonizing the beginning of the calendar year with the Amenist theological preamble that God created himself out of nothing; hence, the recurring analogy of the Sun emerging from the primordial ocean.

**Stage 2:** The virtual death of the soul to the realm of spirit upon its entrance into a human host. The Litany of Ra states:

> *". . . Ra gives birth to the royal [[Osir]] (i.e., the Pharaoh), he causes his own birth."*[43]

Amenism teaches that Osir, ". . . whose complexion is black, and who is described by one of his many titles as the 'Great Black One,'" became the first king of Kemet and traveled the world transmitting civilization to all nations, but that he was killed by his evil brother Seth who sealed him in a wooden chest ". . . and then threw the chest into the Nile River where Osir suffered death by drowning."[44] Annual pilgrimages to the holy city of Abydos, where the tomb of Osir was located and was reportedly discovered by French archaeologist Emile Amelineau, were made by the faithful to engage in worship, and to set up ". . . offering tablets . . . inscribed with their names and prayers" during the events of the passion play of Osir called "mysteries," which was a part of the annual festival of Osir that took place over a period of 14 days beginning on the seventeenth day of the month of Ka Hera Ka (**KA HAIR**-uh **KA**) or November 8th (Gregorian), as *encryptedly* reported by Greek biographer Plutarch who said that Osir was murdered "upon the 17th day of the month Athyr (*i.e.*, Het-Heru), when the sun was in Scorpio," which from the standpoint of the Kemetan calendar and Zodiac is in reference to: 1) the aforementioned annual reenactment of the suffering, death, revival and resurrection or passion play of Osir that did in fact begin on the **17th day**, but in the month of Ka Hera Ka, and when the Sun was in Virgo, 2) the <u>symbolic</u> death of Osir as the personification of the falling Nile that was in fact observed on **17th day** of the **month of Het-Heru**, but when the Sun was in Libra, and 3) the <u>actual</u> death of Osir that did in fact occur when the **Sun was in Scorpio**, but in the month of Paen Aopet (**PAH**-en **OH**-pet) (*see* Plate 1).[45]

*Volumes*, Volume I, (London: John Murray, 1920), 321b.

    43. Edouard Naville, "The Litany of Ra," in *Records of the Past*, Volume VIII, Egyptian Texts, ed. Samuel Birch, (London: Samuel Bagster and Sons, 1874), 124. Mine in parentheses. Italics mine. [[ ]] Double brackets indicate word or term substitution made by the author. Here, the spelling of the name "Osir," which refers to the first person of God Ra, is consistent with the teachings of Amenism and has therefore been substituted for the name "Osiris," which is Greek.

    44. Tarík Karenga, *The Pharaohs' 5 Laws of Success*, First Edition, (Union City: Amenism, Inc., 2022), 15-16. The Nile River reached its highest point near the end of September when Osir was drowned. Rushdi Said, *The River Nile: Geology, Hydrology and Utilization*, (Tarrytown: Pergamon Press, 1993), 96. "(T)he Nile is at its lowest level in the months of May and June . . ." Marc Van De Mieroop, *A History of Ancient Egypt*, (Malden: Wiley-Blackwell, 2011), 8. Capitalization mine. *See* also Plate 1.

    45. Zahi Hawass and Sandro Vannini, *The Lost Tombs of Thebes: Life in Paradise*, (London: Thames & Hudson, 2009), 173. Cheikh Anta Diop, *The African Origin of Civilization: Myth or Reality*, (Chicago: Lawrence Hill Books, 1974), 75. Pat Remler, *Egyptian Mythology A to Z*, Third Edition, (New York: Chelsea House Publishers, 2010), 3. E. A. Wallis Budge, *Egyptian Ideas of the Future Life*, Second Edition, (London: Kegan Paul, Trench, Trubner & Co., Ltd., 1900), 46. Mine in parentheses. The period of 14 days symbolizes ". . . the 14 days of the waning moon" as well as the fourteen pieces into which Osir was cut by his evil brother Seth. *See* George St. Clair, *Creation Records Discovered in Egypt: Studies in the Book of the Dead*, (London: David Nutt, 1898), 249. According to Greek biographer Plutarch, at the time of the annual Festi-

In the Kemetan Mystery System, which is permeated with the religion of Amenism, the divine births, lives and deaths of subsequent kings of Kemet (*i.e.*, Pharaohs) were seen in the divine birth, life and death of Osir and his son Heru with whom they all were identified, because just like Osir and Heru who had both come into the world by way of a divine birth, so too was every king ". . . said to have had a divine birth, having been begotten of spirit and born of a *Virgin Mother* by whom the king had been divinely conceived when his then virgin mother-to-be was descended upon by God Amen himself."[46] Yet, on analogy with the teaching that Osir had been sealed in a wooden chest, cast into the Nile River and suffered death by drowning, the Pharaohs and other Initiates of the Mystery System came to regard "the human body ("approximately 75 percent water") as a prison house of the soul," wherein the soul experiences what is known as *spiritual slumber i.e.*, "the sleeplike state of the soul resembling *spiritual death*, characterized by restricted mobility that accompanies the inhabitation of the spiritually unborn and immaterial living soul in a physical body where it is virtually imprisoned <u>spiritually</u> and <u>experientially</u> one step removed from *true life*."[47] So from the perspective of the Pharaoh, the theology of his divine birth from a *Virgin Mother* was understood philosophically as his ". . . coming into biological life spiritually and experientially one step removed from the realm of spirit by means of the birth of . . ." his physical body that he, "the spiritually unborn and immaterial living soul," inhabited (*see* Table 8).[48]

The actual death of Osir, which in the Mysteries is seen also as the death of the Sun *i.e.*, the virtual death of the soul to the realm of spirit, is officially observed at **twelve o'clock midnight** on the thirtieth day of the month of Paen Aopet or September 22nd (Gregorian) when the Sun is in the zodiacal sign Scorpio, which is interpreted also as **twelve o'clock in the morning** on the first day of the month of Het-Heru (**HET** hay-**ROO**) or September 23rd (Gregorian) when the Sun is moving out of Scorpio and into Libra, marking the official observance date of the divine birth of the Pharaoh, and symbolically representing the Pharaoh's *spiritual crucifixion* by way of analogizing the death of Osir by drowning while sealed in a wooden chest to the entrance or crossing over of the soul into a human host, which corresponds to the astronomical event of the fall (*i.e.*, autumnal) equinox when ". . . the Sun crosses (the

___

val of Osir "nights grow longer." Also, during the reenactment of the passion play of Osir, the body of Osir disappeared and was found after three days; then, shouts of joy rang out that "Osir has been found;" Osir had <u>spiritually</u> "risen from the dead." D. M. Murdock, *Christ in Egypt: The Horus-Jesus Connection*, (Seattle: Stellar House Publishing, 2009), 69 and (note 4), 103, 380-382. According to Amenism, Osir was found and spiritually revived at **twelve o'clock midnight** on Ta Aobyti 29th or December 20th (Gregorian), he was entombed at **twelve o'clock midnight** on Paen Renñutet 26th, and he was resurrected three days later at **twelve o'clock in the morning** on Paen Renñutet 30th (which is also **twelve o'clock midnight** on the previous day); notwithstanding, the reenactment of these important events took place during the month of Ka Hera Ka. *See* also Budge, *op. cit.*, Gods, Volume II, 1904, 123. The Nile receded in mid-October; Marc Van De Mieroop, *A History of Ancient Egypt*, (Malden: Wiley-Blackwell, 2011), 8. *See* "Stage 3" and "Stage 4" below.

46. Tarík Karenga, *The Pharaohs' 5 Laws of Success*, First Edition, (Union City: Amenism, Inc., 2022), 17-18.

47. George G. M. James, *Stolen Legacy*, (Trenton: African World Press, 1992), 1. In parentheses *see* Pat Remler, *Egyptian Mythology A to Z*, Third Edition, (New York: Chelsea House Publishers, 2010), 125. *See* the terms *spiritual death* and *spiritual slumber*, in Tarík Karenga, *Review of the Kemetan Mystery System*, First Edition, (Union City: Amenism, Inc., in press).

48. Tarík Karenga, *The Pharaohs' 5 Laws of Success*, First Edition, (Union City: Amenism, Inc., 2022), 20. *See* the term *divine birth*, in Tarík Karenga, *Review of the Kemetan Mystery System*, First Edition, (Union City: Amenism, Inc., in press). The soul preexisted the creation of the body and exercised free will in choosing to come down to earth.

equator) from the northern into the southern celestial hemisphere," during the course of which "day and night are of equal length," but "thereafter nights steadily grow longer" than days (*see* Plates 1 and 3).[49] So it is the case that knowledge of the equinoxes as well as of the solstices was employed to synchronize the calendar with the seasons.

Equally important; however, was the daily observation of the brightest fixed star in the heavens called Sepdta (**SEP**-tah) (Sothis in Greek and Sirius in English), which was not only identified with Iset, but was also the herald of the birth of Heru (as a newborn babe), as in the Northern Hemisphere Sepdta can be seen annually during midwinter rising in the east; however, for a period of **seventy days**, officially observed from the eleventh day of the month of Ap Ap (**AHP AHP**) through the fifteenth day of the month of Tekhi (**TEK**-ee), or May 31st through August 8th (Gregorian), Sepdta disappears "due to (solar glare from) being too close to the Sun," and during the entire period of which the body of the deceased and *former* Pharaoh was said to have been embalmed and prepared for entombment before the first appearance of Sepdta that in ancient Kemet took place on the sixteenth day of the month of Tekhi or August 9th (Gregorian) and "coincided with the flooding of the Nile," as the annual first appearance (*i.e.*, heliacal rising) of Sepdta occurred exactly one day before the Nile reached a favorable level ". . . for the inundation of the basin lands of Egypt . . ." as determined by measurements made by priests, and at which point on the seventeenth day of the month of Tekhi or August 10th (Gregorian), canals would be opened to allow the Nile water to overflow the plain, which was indispensable to the agriculture of Kemet (*see* Plate 1).[50] Note that in actuality the annual heliacal rising of Sepdta takes place

49. Ernest Busenbark, *Symbols, Sex, and the Stars in Popular Beliefs*, (New York: The Truth Seeker Company, Inc., 1949), viii, 117, 122, 124. Eric Chaisson and Steve McMillan, *Astronomy: A Beginner's Guide to the Universe*, Fifth Edition, (Upper Saddle River: Pearson Prentice Hall, 2007), 11. Mine in parentheses. Sun Kwok, *Our Place in the Universe: Understanding Fundamental Astronomy from Ancient Discoveries*, Second Edition, (Cham: Springer International Publishing AG, 2017), 12. *See* also D. M. Murdock, *Christ in Egypt: The Horus-Jesus Connection*, (Seattle: Stellar House Publishing, 2009), 356-357, 359, 396. Logan Mitchell, *Religion in the Heavens; Or, Mythology Unveiled*, (London: Freethought Publishing Company, 1881), 95. In the Mysteries, Het-Heru is identified with Iset, and like Iset, she is said to be the mother of Heru. *Ibid.*, 148, 178-181. E. A. Wallis Budge, *Egyptian Ideas of the Future Life*, Second Edition, (London: Kegan Paul, Trench, Trubner & Co., Ltd., 1900), 46. *See* also E. A. Wallis Budge, *An Egyptian Hieroglyphic Dictionary: In Two Volumes*, Volume I, (London: John Murray, 1920), 236a-b. *See* also "equinox" in Webster's New World Dictionary & Thesaurus, Version 2.0, Build #25, Accent Software International, Macmillan Publishers, 1998. A plagiarized, adapted and reconfigured version of this Amenist teaching is in the religion of Christianity. *See* The Holy Bible: *Comprising the Old and New Testaments*, The King James Version, (New York: American Bible Society, 1972), [(NT) Matthew 27:32-56], 32-33; [Mark 15:21-41], 54-55; [Luke 23:26-43], 90-91; [Revelation 11:8], 254. *See* the terms *divine birth* and *spiritual crucifixion*, in Tarík Karenga, *Review of the Kemetan Mystery System*, First Edition, (Union City: Amenism, Inc., in press).

50. Robert Burnham, Jr., *Burnham's Celestial Handbook: An Observer's Guide to the Universe Beyond the Solar System*, Volume I, Revised and Enlarged Edition, (Mineola: Dover Publications, Inc., 1978), 387, 391. Heliacal rising is defined as: "When a star rises on the eastern horizon before sunrise for the first time following a solar conjunction," and based on the above official observance dates for the first appearance and the disappearance of Sepdta, a solar conjunction (*i.e.*, the conjunction of Sepdta and the Sun) takes place on the tenth day of the month of Mesut Ra (**MAY-SOOT RAH**) or July 4th (Gregorian) when the Sun is in the zodiacal sign Capricorn. The exact date of the annual heliacal rising of Sepdta was on August 5th in the year 2017 C.E. as reported by Astronomer Sun Kwok, which means that in the year 2000 at the beginning of a Sepdtaic cycle that occurred in a calendar year whose first day of the first month coincided with the beginning of a "Great Year" cycle, the date of the heliacal rising of Sepdta was on the sixteenth day of the month of Tekhi or August 9th (Gregorian), the same date observed by our ancient Kemetan ancestors; additionally, that the annual heliacal rising of Sepdta takes place a day earlier every 4 years, there are records that place this momentous event on the first day of the first month of

a day earlier every 4 years and therefore reoccurs on the sixteenth day of the month of Tekhi only every 1,460 years, which is known as the **Sepdtaic** (sep-**TAY**-ic) **cycle**; nevertheless, the official observance date of the annual first appearance (*i.e.*, heliacal rising) of Sepdta has been fixed on the Kemetan calendar for contemporary practical purposes.[51]

**Stage 3:** The birth of the soul characterized by its emergence above its human host, ". . . directly into the realm of spirit."[52] The Litany of Ra says:

> *"Oh, Ra, come to the King! Truly. Thou makest thy*
>
> *soul young again and thou givest birth to thy body."*[53]

According to the religion of Amenism, after the death of Osir his wife Iset, who was also his sister, not ". . . by blood, but rather by spirit," recovered the body of Osir and transported it back to Kemet where Seth ". . . regained possession of his brother's body by chance and . . . cut it into fourteen pieces which he scattered (and buried) far and wide."[54] Iset, determined to find the "precious fragments" of her

the year (*i.e.*, New Year's Day) and around the time of the summer solstice; however, the original first appearance of Sepdta, which was also the beginning of the first Sepdtaic cycle following Zep Tepi, and the beginning of the first "Great Year" cycle, occurred on the sixteenth day of the month of Tekhi or August 9th (Gregorian). *See* Table 7 below. *See* also Sun Kwok, *Our Place in the Universe: Understanding Fundamental Astronomy from Ancient Discoveries*, Second Edition, (Cham: Springer International Publishing AG, 2017), 26, 29, 84, 125, 256. Mine in parentheses. Rosemary Clark, *The Sacred Magic of Ancient Egypt*, (St. Paul: Llewellyn Publications, 2003), 116 (note 2). According to Amenism, the first day beginning at the end of the five-day summer solstice period (*e.g.*, June 25th) when the Sun ". . . reverses its movement and **begins to *visibly rise increasingly southward* . . .**" marks the beginning of the Kemetan calendar year, whereas the heliacal rising of Sepdta at the beginning of each Sepdtaic cycle occurs on the sixteenth day of the month of Tekhi or August 9th (Gregorian), which has become its annual official observance date. *See* "Stage 1" above. R. J. Condon, *Our Pagan Christmas*, (Austin: American Atheist Press, 1989), 5. D. M. Murdock, *Christ in Egypt: The Horus-Jesus Connection*, (Seattle: Stellar House Publishing, 2009), 205. Cheikh Anta Diop, *Civilization or Barbarism: An Authentic Anthropology*, (Brooklyn: Lawrence Hill Books, 1991), 279. Norman Lockyer, *The Dawn of Astronomy: A Study of the Temple-Worship and Mythology of the Ancient Egyptians*, (London: Cassell and Company Limited, 1894), 194-197. James P. Allen, *Middle Egyptian: An Introduction to the Language and Culture of Hieroglyphs*, (New York: Cambridge University Press, 2001), 94, 105. Eric Orlin, ed., *The Routledge Encyclopedia of Ancient Mediterranean Religions*, (New York: Routledge, 2016), 103. E. A. Wallis Budge, *The Mummy: A Handbook of Egyptian Funerary Archaeology*, Second Edition, Revised & Greatly Enlarged, (London: Cambridge University Press, 1925), 342. E. A. Wallis Budge, *An Egyptian Hieroglyphic Dictionary: In Two Volumes*, Volume II, (London: John Murray, 1920), 664a. "The level of 16 cubits was the level most favorable for the inundation of the basin lands of Egypt during Graeco-Roman time and also at the beginning of the Arab period . . ." Rushdi Said, *The River Nile: Geology, Hydrology and Utilization*, (Tarrytown: Pergamon Press, 1993), 98. Sir J. Gardner Wilkinson, *The Manners and Customs of the Ancient Egyptians*, Volume II, (London: John Murray, 1878), 365 and (note 1), 429. For some of the principal productions of ancient Kemet that were made possible as a result of the annual inundation of the Nile River *see ibid.*, 398-427.

51. Rosemary Clark, *The Sacred Magic of Ancient Egypt*, (St. Paul: Llewellyn Publications, 2003), 116 (note 2). The Sepdtaic cycle is defined as the time interval of 1,460 years between two heliacal risings of Sepdta on the sixteenth day of the month of Tekhi.

52. Tarík Karenga, *The Pharaohs' 5 Laws of Success*, First Edition, (Union City: Amenism, Inc., 2022), 17, 20. *See* the term *spiritual rebirth*, in Tarík Karenga, *Review of the Kemetan Mystery System*, First Edition, (Union City: Amenism, Inc., in press).

53. Edouard Naville, "The Litany of Ra," in *Records of the Past*, Volume VIII, Egyptian Texts, ed. Samuel Birch, (London: Samuel Bagster and Sons, 1874), 119. Italics mine.

54. Tarík Karenga, *The Pharaohs' 5 Laws of Success*, First Edition, (Union City: Amenism, Inc., 2022), 16, 25-26. Felix Guirand, *Larousse Encyclopedia of Mythology*, (New York: Prometheus Press, 1960), 18. Mine in parentheses. Greek

husband's body was, after a three-day search that began at **twelve o'clock midnight** on the twenty-sixth day of the month of Ta Aobyti (**TAH** oh-**BIT**-ee) or December 17th (Gregorian), able to recover ". . . them all except the phallus which had been greedily devoured by a Nile crab, the Oxyrhynchid, forever accursed for this crime."[55] So, she, "the great virgin," not only rejoined the body of and spiritually revived Osir, but with him Iset also conjoined in spirit while she ". . . spiritually drew from Osir his essence and conceived a divine child" who she affectionately named Heru, the very person who the Pharaoh was said to be.[56] Hence, the Pharaoh occupied the throne by virtue of his identification with Osir, but he ruled his earthly kingdom ". . . as the Son of God and third person of the Holy Trinity: Heru."[57]

The conception of Heru whereupon he subsequently entered the "birth-chamber" of his virgin mother Iset is officially observed at **twelve o'clock midnight** on the thirtieth day of the month of Ta Aobyti or December 21st (Gregorian) when the Sun is in the zodiacal sign Leo, which besides having fallen on the shortest day of the year *i.e.*, the day of the winter solstice, exactly three days later, on the fourth day of the month of Makhiar or on ". . . the morning of December 25th" when the Sun was in the zodiacal sign Kheper, Heru was born, which in the Mysteries was seen also as the new birth of the Sun *i.e.*, the newborn soul (*see* Table 4, and Plates 1 and 3).[58]

biographer Plutarch states that "The dismemberment of Osiris into fourteen parts they refer allegorically to the days of the waning of that satellite from the time of the full moon to the new moon . . ." Plutarch also states that the fragments of Osir's body had not only been scattered, but that they had also been buried. D. M. Murdock, *Christ in Egypt: The Horus-Jesus Connection*, (Ashland: Stellar House Publishing, 2009), 70, 379.

    55. Tarík Karenga, *The Pharaohs' 5 Laws of Success*, First Edition, (Union City: Amenism, Inc., 2022), 16. Felix Guirand, *Larousse Encyclopedia of Mythology*, (New York: Prometheus Press, 1960), 18. *See* also Susie M. Best, *World Famous Stories in Historic Settings: Egypt and Her Neighbors*, (New York: The Macmillan Company, 1918), 45. "Osiris in his maimed and mutilated state was represented by the child of Isis, the Horus of twelve years, or the moon in the fourteen days of waning light, or the sun in the winter solstice." Gerald Massey, *Ancient Egypt: The Light of the World*, Volume II, (London: T. Fisher Unwin, 1907), 796. Greek biographer Plutarch states: "During this period when Isis was said to be in search of Osiris, the god was claimed to be dead and buried for three days . . . and, on the fourth, he is called out by his son, Horus." D. M. Murdock, *Christ in Egypt: The Horus-Jesus Connection*, (Ashland: Stellar House Publishing, 2009), 379. The method for reckoning the three days; *see, ibid.*, 83. Nile flood stage officially ends at midnight on Ta Aobyti 29th or December 20th (Gregorian), though the Nile receded between mid-October and November *(see Plate 1)*. *See* also Rushdi Said, *The River Nile: Geology, Hydrology and Utilization*, (Tarrytown: Pergamon Press, 1993), 96. Marc Van De Mieroop, *A History of Ancient Egypt*, (Malden: Wiley-Blackwell, 2011), 8. *See* also Colonel Sir Scott Moncrieff, "Engineering," in *Nature* 72, no. 1871, ed. Sir Norman Lockyer, (London: MacMillan and Co., Limited, 1905): 468. According to Greek biographer Plutarch, during the reenactment of the passion play of Osir, the body of Osir disappeared and was found after three days; then, shouts of joy rang out that "Osir has been found;" Osir had spiritually "risen from the dead." Murdock, *op. cit.*, 2009, p. 380-382. According to Amenism, Osir was found and spiritually revived at **twelve o'clock midnight** on Ta Aobyti 29th or December 20th (Gregorian), he was entombed at **twelve o'clock midnight** on Paen Renñutet 26th, and he was resurrected three days later at **twelve o'clock in the morning** on Paen Renñutet 30th (which is also **twelve o'clock midnight** on the previous day); notwithstanding, the reenactment of these important events took place during the month of Ka Hera Ka. *See* "Stage 4" below.

    56. Tarík Karenga, *The Pharaohs' 5 Laws of Success*, First Edition, (Union City: Amenism, Inc., 2022), 16-17. *See* the term *spiritual revival*, in Tarík Karenga, *Review of the Kemetan Mystery System*, First Edition, (Union City: Amenism, Inc., in press).

    57. Tarík Karenga, *The Pharaohs' 5 Laws of Success*, First Edition, (Union City: Amenism, Inc., 2022), 19.

    58. Ernest Busenbark, *Symbols, Sex, and the Stars in Popular Beliefs*, (New York: The Truth Seeker Company, Inc., 1949), 116-117. Eric Chaisson and Steve McMillan, *Astronomy: A Beginner's Guide to the Universe*, Fifth Edition, (Upper Saddle River: Pearson Prentice Hall, 2007), 10. *See* also "solstice" in *Webster's New World Dictionary & Thesaurus*, Version 2.0, Build #25, Accent Software International, Macmillan Publishers, 1998. The birth-chamber of Iset as seen from the perspective of Osir is called the *"cradle of Osir"* in which he ". . . renews his birth" as Heru. D. M. Murdock, *Christ in*

The above events, that is, the conception and birth of Heru (as a newborn babe), correspond to the astronomical event in which the Sun, having appeared to stand still or rise from the same spot for approximately three days in a row during the period of the *winter solstice* and at its apparent maximum distance south of the celestial equator, reverses its movement and **begins to *visibly* rise increasingly northward**, officially observed on the fourth day of the month of Makhiar or December 25th (Gregorian), which is the date of the birth of Heru, and which is called the "Day of the Great Coming Forth."[59]

**Table 4:**                          **The Three-Day Winter Solstice Period**

| Date | Description | |
|---|---|---|
| | Date — Description header | |
| Ta Aobyti 30 | The three-day winter solstice period begins at midnight on the day of the winter solstice and on this day at **twelve o'clock midnight** Heru was conceived, whereupon he subsequently entered the birth-chamber of his virgin mother Iset. The many titles of Iset include: ***"The Lady of the Birth-chamber"***[60] and ***"Chamber-of-the-Birth-of-a-God."***[61] | Dec 21 |
| Makhiar 1 | From midnight on Ta Aobyti 30th to midnight on Makhiar 1st constitutes the first day of the three-day winter solstice period and Heru's 1st full day in the birth-chamber of his virgin mother Iset. | Dec 22 |
| Makhiar 2 | From midnight on Makhiar 1st to midnight on Makhiar 2nd constitutes the second day of the three-day winter solstice period and Heru's 2nd full day in the birth-chamber of his virgin mother Iset. | Dec 23 |

---

*Egypt: The Horus-Jesus Connection*, (Seattle: Stellar House Publishing, 2009), 140. *See* also Sir P. Le Page Renouf and Prof. E. Naville, *The Egyptian Book of the Dead: Translation and Commentary*, (London: The Society of Biblical Archaeology, 1904), 131-132. *See* also, E. A. Wallis Budge, *The Gods of the Egyptians: Or, Studies in Egyptian Mythology*, Volume II, (London: Methuen & Company, 1904), 293 (note 4). *See* also E. A. Wallis Budge, *An Egyptian Hieroglyphic Dictionary: In Two Volumes*, Volume I, (London: John Murray, 1920), 286a. *See* also E. A. Wallis Budge, *The Mummy: A Handbook of Egyptian Funerary Archaeology*, Second Edition, Revised & Greatly Enlarged, (London: Cambridge University Press, 1925), 481. Tarík Karenga, *The Pharaohs' 5 Laws of Success*, First Edition, (Union City: Amenism, Inc., 2022), 21.

    59. D. M. Murdock, *Christ in Egypt: The Horus-Jesus Connection*, (Seattle: Stellar House Publishing, 2009), 83, 104-106 and (note 1). *See* also "solstice" in Webster's New World Dictionary & Thesaurus, Version 2.0, Build #25, Accent Software International, Macmillan Publishers, 1998. That the day of the winter solstice is the shortest day of the year, the period of the winter solstice is two days shorter than that of the summer solstice. According to the teachings of the religion of Amenism. *See* also Tarík Karenga, *The Pharaohs' 5 Laws of Success*, First Edition, (Union City: Amenism, Inc., 2022), 19.

    60. E. A. Wallis Budge, *Osiris and the Egyptian Resurrection*, Volume II, (New York: G. P. Putnam's Sons, 1911), 277. Italics mine.

    61. Eloise McKinney-Johnson, "Egypt's Isis: The Original Black Madonna," in *Black Women in Antiquity*, ed. Ivan Van Sertima, (New Brunswick: Transaction Publishers, 1988), 64.

| Makhiar 3 | From midnight on Makhiar 2nd to midnight on Makhiar 3rd, which is also the morning of Makhiar 4th or December 25th (Gregorian), constitutes the third day of the three-day winter solstice period and Heru's 3rd full day in the birth-chamber of his virgin mother Iset. | Dec 24 |
|---|---|---|

Having given birth to Heru on the fourth day of the month of Makhiar or December 25th (Gregorian), the second person of the Holy Trinity Iset:

*". . . hid him carefully, so that [[Seth]] might not find him.*

*But during her absence in the city of Am, where she had gone*

*to buy food, [[Seth,]] in the form of a scorpion, found the child and*

*stung him, and when [[Iset]] returned she found him lying dead."*[62]

So Iset raised her voice unto heaven where her supplication reached the Boat of Eternity and the Sun descended ". . . in its journeying, and (for a period of one day) moved not from the place whereon it rested."[63] Then, Tekhi, the Ibis-headed form of Amen and "herald of the gods" who is reputed to have ". . . reckoned the time, the years and the calendar and controlled the divisions of time," leaped down from the Boat of Eternity and assured Iset that the Sun "is in the (same) place where it was yesterday," and that Kemet would remain in darkness until Heru was made whole.[64] That being said, Tekhi forthwith taught Iset ". . . certain words of power and how to use them, and as soon as she uttered them over [[Heru]], the child was restored to life. [[Tekhi]] ascended into the sky and took his place in the Boat, and the Sun-god (Ra) resumed his journey."[65]

---

62. E. A. Wallis Budge, *Legends of Our Lady Mary the Perpetual Virgin and Her Mother Hanna*, (London: The Medici Society, 1922), liii. Italics mine. [[ ]] Double brackets indicate word or term substitution made by the author. Here, the spellings of the names "Iset" and "Seth" are consistent with the teachings of Amenism and have therefore been substituted for the names "Isis" (Greek) and "Set" (variation of Seth).

63. In his reference notes, E. A. Wallis Budge states that the Disk or Sun "alighted." *See* E. A. Wallis Budge, *Legends of the Egyptian Gods: Hieroglyphic Texts and Translations*, (New York: Dover Publications, Inc., 1994), 187. Mine in parentheses. Adolf Erman, *A Handbook of Egyptian Religion*, (London: Archibald Constable & CO. LTD., 1907), 152. *See* also E. A. Wallis Budge, *The Literature of the Ancient Egyptians*, (London: J. M. Dent & Sons Limited, 1914), 91.

64. E. A. Wallis Budge, *The Literature of the Ancient Egyptians*, (London: J. M. Dent & Sons Limited, 1914), 91. Mine in parentheses. *See* also Adolf Erman, *A Handbook of Egyptian Religion*, (London: Archibald Constable & CO. LTD., 1907), 152. *See* also Ahmed Abuelgasim Elhassan, *Religious Motifs in Meroitic Painted and Stamped Pottery*, (Oxford: John and Erica Hedges Ltd., 2004), 24. Felix Guirand, *Larousse Encyclopedia of Mythology*, (New York: Prometheus Press, 1960), 27. The "Boat of Eternity" is the Boat of Ra in which the Sun was said to travel across the sky each day.

65. E. A. Wallis Budge, *Legends of Our Lady Mary the Perpetual Virgin and Her Mother Hanna*, (London: The Medici Society, 1922), liii. Mine in parentheses. [[ ]] Double brackets indicate word or term substitution made by the author. Here, the spellings of the names "Heru" and "Tekhi" are consistent with the teachings of Amenism and have therefore been substituted for the names "Horus" and "Thoth," which are both Greek.

In the Mystery System, to halt the Sun for one day is tantamount to adding a day to the calendar and postponing *regularly scheduled* activities for the intervening twenty-four hour period; hence, it takes no stretch of the imagination to understand why in ancient times, after falling under Greek rule, we obstinately rebelled against the Decree of Canopus made by Ptolemy III, Euergetes I, who attempted to usurp an institution that in the Mysteries had already been established by God; namely, the age-old institution of keeping the calendar in sync with the seasons by adding a day to the calendar every fourth year at the end of the month of Makhiar.[66] This is known as a leap year and because it had been instituted by God, the oath made by Kemetan kings ". . . at the moment of their accession not to alter the year" consequently was not violated.[67]

True, previous investigations of ancient Kemetan culture found that there were at least three types of calendars in use simultaneously, but of those discussed, none were said to have included a set of rules that required a day to be added to the calendar every fourth year. Moreover, Egyptologist Dr. Cheikh Anta Diop tells us that on the contrary our African ancestors of ancient Kemet ". . . preferred to 'rectify' every 1,460 years instead of every 4 years . . . (which) is the lapse of time that separates two heliacal risings of Sirius (*i.e.*, Sepdta)" on the sixteenth day of the month of Tekhi.[68] Notwithstanding the Sepdtaic cycle, we learn from ancient Greek historian Herodotus that the Kemetans,

*". . . dividing the year into twelve months of thirty days each,*

*add every year a space of five days besides, whereby the circuit*

*of the seasons is made to return with uniformity."*[69]

The above could only have occurred if the ancient Kemetans were in fact adding a day to the calendar every 4 years, because without doing so would have resulted in the actual seasons advancing **.2422** of a day ahead of the calendrical seasons every year, and almost a day (**.9688**) ahead of the calendrical seasons every 4 years, which recalls to mind that more than 1,000 years before Herodotus traveled to Kemet ". . . the bringing of the 'two great obelisks' from the granite quarries of Aswan to Thebes . . ." by Sen-Mut (**SEN**-moot), the architect of Pharaoh Queen Hatshepsut (hat-**SHEP**-soot), not only demonstrated the skill and mastery of the workforce, but it also suggested that a set of rules was being utilized to

66. James Henry Breasted, "The Beginnings of Time-Measurement and the Origins of Our Calendar," in *Time and Its Mysteries: Series 1*, (Washington Square: New York University Press, 1936), 74. "Thoth . . . travels in the Solar Boat . . . jumping out every fourth (leap) year for one day." H. P. Blavatsky, *The Secret Doctrine*, Volume II, Third and Revised Edition, (London: The Theosophical Publishing House, 1893), 558. *See* also Plate 1.

67. Juan Antonio Belmonte, "The Egyptian Calendar: Keeping Ma'at on Earth," in *In Search of Cosmic Order: Selected Essays on Egyptian Archaeoastronomy*, eds. Juan Antonio Belmonte and Mosalam Shaltout, (Cairo: Supreme Council of Antiquities, 2009), 79.

68. According to Amenism, the preference for rectifying every 1,460 years helped to keep secret the knowledge of rectifying every 4 years. *See* Cheikh Anta Diop, *Civilization or Barbarism: An Authentic Anthropology*, (Brooklyn: Lawrence Hill Books, 1991), 279-280. Mine in parentheses. The duration of a tropical year (or solar year) is equal to 365.2422 days. *Ibid.*, 401-402 (note 63).

69. George Rawlinson, *History of Herodotus*, In Four Volumes, Volume II, (London: John Murray, 1862), 3-4.

keep the calendar in sync with the seasons of the year and those rules, as we have seen, were masterfully hidden within the teachings of the Mysteries.[70] Pharaoh Queen Hatshepsut says:

*"My Majesty began to work on them on the first day of the second month of the*

*season of Pert (i.e., on Paen Khonsu 1st in the season of growing and harvesting),*

*of the fifteenth year of my reign, and continued so to do until the last day of the*

*fourth month of the season Shemut (i.e., Het-Heru 30th in the season of inundation),*

*in the sixteenth year of my reign, that is to say, the work lasted seven months*

*from the time when it was begun in the mountain [at Aswan]."*[71]  (*See* Plate 1).

This brings us to the second rule of the Kemetan calendar; which, having only the first rule in place results in the calendrical seasons advancing **.0312** of a day ahead of the actual seasons every 4 years as with the Julian calendar, which is yet another reconfigured version of our own.[72]  Nevertheless, unlike the Julian calendar that fell more and more out of sync with the seasons as its calendrical seasons advanced almost a day (**.9984**) ahead of the actual seasons every 128 years, the Kemetan calendar, as its second rule, **does not** add a day for years that are divisible by 128, unless the same year is also divisible by 80,000.[73]  Consequently, the actual seasons begin to advance just **.0016** of a day ahead of the calendrical seasons every 128 years and **exactly one day** ahead of the calendrical seasons every 80,000 years, at which point **exactly one day** is added to the calendar, bringing the differential to **0**, which in turn brings the Kemetan calendar back into <u>absolute</u> perfect sync with the seasons as it was at "Zep Tepi," meaning the *first time* and which refers to the moment of creation in remote antiquity when ". . . the

---

70. E. A. Wallis Budge, *A History of Egypt*, Volume IV, (New York: Oxford University Press, 1902), 15.

71. *Ibid.*, 18-19. Mine in parentheses. Italics mine. Beginning the work on Paen Khonsu 1st, it would have taken at least two or three months in the season of Pert ". . . to cut the blocks out of their beds in the quarry . . ." and since the Nile River began to rise shortly thereafter on the birthday of Osir on Oup Renpet 1st, the blocks would have needed to be transported to and loaded aboard the ships before the Nile reached a height which permitted the floating of the two massive blocks down the river. Finally, it would have taken the two or three remaining months in the season of Shemu to erect and inscribe the "two great obelisks" by Het-Heru 30th. *See* also E. A. Wallis Budge, *Facsimiles of Egyptian Hieratic Papyri in the British Museum*, Series 1, (London: Oxford University Press, 1910), xvi.

72. Sacha Stern, *Calendars in Antiquity: Empires, States, and Societies*, (Oxford: Oxford University Press, 2012), 211-212.

73. There is no reason why the ancient Kemetans would not have known about *rule two* when one considers that the calendar that was in sync with the seasons during the reign of Pharaoh Queen Hatshepsut was the same calendar that was in sync with the seasons when Greek historian Herodotus traveled to Kemet more than 1,000 years later. In the year 1869 (Gregorian), author Edmund Denison proposed that losing a leap day every 128 years should be considered as a second rule for the Julian calendar; however, his proposal never gained any traction. *See* Edmund Beckett Denison, *Astronomy Without Mathematics*, (New York: G. P. Putnam & Sons, 1869), 123. Prior to the Julian calendar, which we have learned is a reconfigured version of the Kemetan calendar, ". . . the Egyptian (*i.e.*, Kemetan) calendar spread and took over the ancient world . . ." *See* Sacha Stern, *Calendars in Antiquity: Empires, States, and Societies*, (Oxford: Oxford University Press, 2012), 127. Mine in parentheses.

present order of the world was definitively distinguished from chaos by the action of the creator god par excellence."[74]  Furthermore, it is equally astonishing that the differential sequence (.2422, .0312, .0016 and 0) subsequently repeats in perpetuity, and that is why Kemetan history begins with **"0"** followed by **"1"** as a symbolic reenactment of this monumental event (Zep Tepi) that brought order to chaos at the time of *creation—out of nothing*.  Truly, there has never been a more superior calendar, nor can there ever be.  Consider the problem of calendar drift solved!  (See Table 5).[75]

**Table 5: Kemetan Calendar Leap Year Method**

| Differential | Year Multiplier | | Year | Product | Leap |
|---|---|---|---|---|---|
| 0 | | | Ñun  0 – 1  *Zep Tepi* | | (*absolute perfect sync*) |
| .2422 | 4 | (*i.e.*, 1x4) | 4 | .9688 | yes |
| .0312 | 32 | (*i.e.*, 4x32) | 128 | .9984 | no |
| .0016 | 625 | (*i.e.*, 128x625) | 80,000 | 1 | yes |
| 0 | *sequence repeats* | | | | (*absolute perfect sync*) |
| .2422 | 4 | (*i.e.*, 1x4) | 80,004 | .9688 | yes |
| .0312 | 32 | (*i.e.*, 4x32) | 80,128 | .9984 | no |
| .0016 | 625 | (*i.e.*, 128x625) | 160,000 | 1 | yes |
| 0 | *sequence repeats* | | | | (*absolute perfect sync*) |

Now, Heru had been extremely vulnerable to personal attacks waged against him by his evil uncle Seth who was described as ". . . the incarnation of the spirit of evil . . . He was rough and wild, his skin was white and his hair was red – an abomination to the Egyptians, who compared it to the pelt of an ass," and to make matters worse, Heru, the proclaimed "baby Sun" and "Child of gold" born in the winter, was brought ". . . into the world, feeble and weak."[76]  Nevertheless, the religion of Amenism informs us that soon after Heru was restored to life from being stung by a scorpion, he (as a child) ". . . set to work to avenge the death of his father . . ." Osir, which culminated in a fierce three-day battle with Seth, the two combatants fighting ". . . in the form of two men" until their vicious contending, during which the testicles of Seth were hacked off and the left eye of Heru was torn out, was terminated by a tribunal of the gods who subsequently condemned Seth as a usurper and declared Heru Lord of all Kemet.[77]

74.  Serge Sauneron and Jean Yoyotte, "La Naissance Du Monde Selon L'Egypte Ancienne," in *Sources Orientales I: La Naissance Du Monde*, eds. Anne-Marie Esnoul, Paul Garelli, Yves Hervouet, Marcel Leibovici, Serge Sauneron and Jean Yoyotte, (Paris: Editions Du Seuil, 1959), 78.  (Translated from the French).

75.  Though already in sync, because of its cyclical nature, the Kemetan calendar returns to a state of <u>absolute</u> perfect sync with the seasons every 80,000 years when the differential is 0.  One of the implications is that losing a leap day for years that are divisible by 128 unless the same year is also divisible by 80,000 is the original *rule two* of the Kemetan calendar as believed by Amenists.  Note: Religion and science, temple and state, are hereby reunited.

76.  Felix Guirand, *Larousse Encyclopedia of Mythology*, (New York: Prometheus Press, 1960), 19.  D. M. Murdock, *Christ in Egypt: The Horus-Jesus Connection*, (Seattle: Stellar House Publishing, 2009), 111-112.  Capitalization mine.  E. A. Wallis Budge, *The Gods of the Egyptians: Or, Studies in Egyptian Mythology*, Volume II, (London: Methuen & Company, 1904), 210.

77.  E. A. Wallis Budge, *The Gods of the Egyptians: Or, Studies in Egyptian Mythology*, Volume I, (London:

In this section, we have thus established two important astrological correspondences. First, it will be of immense help to know that during the Greek occupation of Kemet, the zodiacal sign Cancer, which has as its symbol the accursed Nile crab, supplanted the original zodiacal sign Kheper whose symbol is the sacred scarab beetle 🪲.[78] "I am Kheper-Ra 🪲 in the morning . . ." says Ra of whom, in turn, it is said:[79]

> *"Homage to thee, Ra ! Supreme power, the beetle that folds his*
>
> *wings, that rests in the empyrean, that is born as his own son."*[80]

Namely, Heru, the third person of the Holy Trinity, who comes forth in the morning as the new-born Sun (*i.e.*, newborn soul), and under the zodiacal sign Kheper, so in this regard Kheper is an emblem of the newborn Sun, which in the Mysteries signifies *spiritual rebirth*.[81] That being said, before proceeding to the second astrological correspondence, it is worth mentioning that the dates assigned to the zodiacal sign Cancer *e.g.*, from the birthday of Heru (as an Elder) on the second day of the **calendrical five-day period** of Oup Renpet or June 21 (Gregorian) through the twenty-eighth day of the month of Mesut Ra or July 22 (Gregorian) are summer months, and therefore as one might expect, the zodiacal sign Kheper, which is instead associated with winter months and with the birth of Heru (as a newborn babe), was not only supplanted by the sign Cancer, but was also assigned new dates; however, this issue has been resolved in the section "The Zodiac."

As regards our second astrological correspondence, the two combatants Heru and Seth bear a demonstrable relationship to the two prominent stars in the constellation Gemini and according to the

Methuen & Company, 1904), 488. Felix Guirand, *Larousse Encyclopedia of Mythology*, (New York: Prometheus Press, 1960), 21-23. J. E. Manchip White, *Ancient Egypt: Its Culture and History*, (New York: Dover Publications Inc., 1970), 31.

78. William Mure, *A Dissertation on the Calendar and Zodiac of Ancient Egypt*, (London: Bell & Bradfute, 1832), 62. *See* also E. A. Wallis Budge, *An Egyptian Hieroglyphic Dictionary: In Two Volumes*, Volume I, (London: John Murray, 1920), 542a, 543a. *See* also Sir W. Drummond, *The Oedipus Judaicus*, (London: A. J. Valpy, Took's Coury, Chancery Lane, 1811), Plates 6-7.

79. Lysander Dickerman, "The Deities of Ancient Egypt," in *The Andover Review: A Religious and Theological Monthly* 3 (January - June 1885): 377 (note 1). Capitalization of the name "Ra" mine. c.f. E. A. Wallis Budge, *Egyptian Magic*, (London: Kegan Paul, Trench, Trubner & Co., Ltd., 1901), 140. Hieroglyphs mine. E. A. Wallis Budge, *The Book of the Dead: The Papyrus of Ani in the British Museum*, (London: Kegan Paul, Trench, Trubner & Co., 1895), 246 (note 2). *See* also E. A. Wallis Budge, *An Egyptian Hieroglyphic Dictionary: In Two Volumes*, Volume I, (London: John Murray, 1920), 542a, 543a-b. *See* also E. A. Wallis Budge, *First Steps in Egyptian: A Book for Beginners*, (London: Kegan Paul, Trench, Trubner & Co., Ltd., 1895), 252.

80. Edouard Naville, "The Litany of Ra," in *Records of the Past*, Volume VIII, Egyptian Texts, ed. Samuel Birch, (London: Samuel Bagster and Sons, 1874), 105. Italics mine.

81. Sir P. Le Page Renouf and Prof. E. Naville, *The Egyptian Book of the Dead: Translation and Commentary*, (London: The Society of Biblical Archaeology, 1904), 222. On the cover of a sarcophagus is depicted "the birth of the Sun as the Winged Scarab at the beginning of the first hour of the day." *Ibid.*, 222. *See* also Auguste Mariette-Bey, *Monuments Divers Recueillis en Egypte et en Nubie*, (Paris: Librairie A. Franck, 1872), Plate 46. The birth of Heru is the new birth of the Sun under the zodiacal sign Kheper. *See* Ippolito Rosellini, *I Monumenti Dell'Egitto e Della Nubia*, Tomo Terzo, Monumenti Del Culto, (Pisa: Presso Niccolo Capurro, 1844), Plate LIII (1). James P. Allen, *The Ancient Egyptian Pyramid Texts*, (Atlanta: Society of Biblical Literature, 2005), 7-8. *See* "Stage 3" above. *See* also Tarík Karenga, *The Pharaohs' 5 Laws of Success*, First Edition, (Union City: Amenism, Inc., 2022), 17, 21.

religion of Amenism, these two stars are actually named after Heru and Seth in view of the fact that the brighter of the "prominent two" (*i.e.*, Heru) is gold in color, while that of the fainter star (Seth) is white.[82] Not surprisingly, the Greeks changed the names of the twin stars from Heru and Seth to the names of the mythological twin brothers Pollux and Castor respectively, but long before the Greeks even existed, Heru, the son of Iset and Osir, often appeared in Kemetan texts as Heru Pikhard *i.e.*, Heru (as a child), and was depicted as such until he miraculously transformed himself ". . . from a child into a man" in order to avenge his father's murder; and that Seth also transformed himself from a *Typhonian animal* ". . . represented as having the features of a fantastic beast with a thin, curved snout, straight, square-cut ears and a stiff forked tail" into a man, the two opponents were figuratively represented as twin combatants/brothers, as well as the twin stars in the constellation Gemini.[83]

Here is one final note. According to the Fourth Sallier Papyrus, the fight between Heru and Seth began ". . . on the 26th day of the month of Thoth (*i.e.*, Tekhi) . . ." but one needs only to remember that such events recorded on the Kemetan calendar are to be kept in chronological order and read as a narrative for optimal results.[84] It is with great pleasure, then, to inform Amenists worldwide that after making several preliminary corrections to the Kemetan calendar and Zodiac, it has been found that rather than having begun on the twenty-sixth day of the month of Tekhi as *encryptedly* reported or purposely shifted out of sequence in the Fourth Sallier Papyrus, the three-day battle between Heru and Seth originally began at **twelve o'clock midnight** on the twenty-sixth day of the month of <u>Paen Amenhotep</u> (**PAH**-en **AMEN**-ho-**TEP**) under the zodiacal sign Gemini, and ended with the defeat of Seth by Heru (as an Elder), who became the "avenger of his father," precisely at **twelve o'clock midnight** exactly three days later, which is interpreted also as **twelve o'clock in the morning** of the thirtieth day of the same month, and this in turn is the same day on which the Sun enters the zodiacal sign Taurus; hence, the Pharaohs delighted in calling themselves "Mighty Bull," and further utilized the title to form their *Heru name*, which was one of the five royal names assumed by the <u>new</u> king upon his accession to the throne on the first day of the tenth month called Paen Khonsu or on March 22nd (Gregorian), which is not surprisingly the same day on which Heru himself became king of all Kemet (*see* Plate 1).[85]

82. Gerald Massey, *Ancient Egypt: The Light of the World*, Volume I, (London: T. Fisher Unwin, 1907), 301,325. *See* also Robert Burnham, Jr., *Burnham's Celestial Handbook: An Observer's Guide to the Universe Beyond the Solar System*, Volume II, Revised and Enlarged Edition, (Mineola: Dover Publications, Inc., 1978), 912.

83. Robert Burnham, Jr., *Burnham's Celestial Handbook: An Observer's Guide to the Universe Beyond the Solar System*, Volume II, Revised and Enlarged Edition, (Mineola: Dover Publications, Inc., 1978), 912. Tarík Karenga, *The Pharaohs' 5 Laws of Success*, First Edition, (Union City: Amenism, Inc., 2022), 17. E. A. Wallis Budge, *The Gods of the Egyptians: Or, Studies in Egyptian Mythology*, Volume I, (London: Methuen & Company, 1904), 486-495. E. A. Wallis Budge, *From Fetish to God in Ancient Egypt*, (New York: Dover Publications, Inc., 1988), 221. *See* also Felix Guirand, *Larousse Encyclopedia of Mythology*, (New York: Prometheus Press, 1960), 20-23, 48. E. A. Wallis Budge, *The Book of the Dead: The Papyrus of Ani in the British Museum*, (London: Kegan Paul, Trench, Trubner & Co., 1895), cxiv-cxv. D. M. Murdock, *Christ in Egypt: The Horus-Jesus Connection*, (Seattle: Stellar House Publishing, 2009), 76.

84. E. A. Wallis Budge, *The Gods of the Egyptians: Or, Studies in Egyptian Mythology*, Volume I, (London: Methuen & Company, 1904), 488.

85. *Ibid.*, 25, 442, 488. E. A. Wallis Budge, *The Mummy: A Handbook of Egyptian Funerary Archaeology*, Second Edition, Revised & Greatly Enlarged, (London: Cambridge University Press, 1925), 359. E. A. Wallis Budge, *The Book of*

We have briefly met with Heru (as a child) and we have since learned of his miraculous transformation from a child into a man, but no sooner did Heru endeavor to avenge his father's murder, than he transformed once again from a man into an Elder, ". . . being that peak stage of development in which he is (symbolically) depicted with the body of a man and the head of a falcon," and it was under this symbolic form that Heru became the vanquisher of Seth and the "avenger of his father" (*see* Plate 4).[86]   In the Mysteries these three latter stages of Heru's development correspond to the three stages of the Pharaoh's *spiritual rebirth* wherein the personal soul emerges ". . . above the flesh, directly into the realm of spirit, rendering one the third person of the Holy Trinity: Heru."[87]  For example, upon entering the first stage titled "Heru (as a child)" the Pharaoh was understandably considered spiritually immature, but had nevertheless experienced and recognized himself as the very person of Heru.  Upon reaching the second stage titled "Heru (as a man)" the Pharaoh was considered spiritually mature, as manhood in fact began at the moment that the Pharaoh consciously and willingly engaged in battle against "evil," or in the language of the ancient Kemetans, "*isfet*."  That is to say, being virtuous, or again, similarly said in the language of the Kemetans, "doing *Maat*" (mah-**AHT**) alone was not enough, for the Pharaoh was charged <u>also</u> with defending the boundaries of *Maat* (*i.e.*, the boundaries of truth, justice, harmony, balance, reciprocity, order, righteousness, wisdom, temperance and courage) against any and all threats to its established laws.[88]  Finally, upon reaching the third stage titled "Heru (as an Elder)" the Pharaoh was considered spiritually equipped and was therefore prepared to carry on in the traditions of his predecessors in general, and to continue the *works of his father* in particular (*see* Table 8).[89]

the Dead: The Papyrus of Ani in the British Museum, (London: Kegan Paul, Trench, Trubner & Co., 1895), cxv. E. A. Wallis Budge, *From Fetish to God in Ancient Egypt*, (New York: Dover Publications, Inc., 1988), 222. cf. Felix Guirand, *Larousse Encyclopedia of Mythology*, (New York: Prometheus Press, 1960), 22. Alan Gardiner, *Egyptian Grammar: Being an Introduction to the Study of Hieroglyphs*, Third Edition, Revised, (Oxford: Griffith Institute, 1994), 71-76. William J. Darby, Paul Ghalioungui and Louis Grivetti, *Food: The Gift of Osiris*, Volume 1, (London: Academic Press, 1977), 321. *See also* "Stage 4" and the section "The Zodiac" below. *See also* E. A. Wallis Budge, *An Egyptian Hieroglyphic Dictionary: In Two Volumes*, Volume I, (London: John Murray, 1920), 236b. The method for reckoning the three days; *see*, D. M. Murdock, *Christ in Egypt: The Horus-Jesus Connection*, (Seattle: Stellar House Publishing, 2009), 83.

86. E. A. Wallis Budge, *The Book of the Dead: The Papyrus of Ani in the British Museum*, (London: Kegan Paul, Trench, Trubner & Co., 1895), cxv. E. A. Wallis Budge, *The Gods of the Egyptians: Or, Studies in Egyptian Mythology*, Volume I, (London: Methuen & Company, 1904), 442, 488. Tarík Karenga, *The Pharaohs' 5 Laws of Success*, First Edition, (Union City: Amenism, Inc., 2022), 17. Mine in parentheses. *See* reference for the *missing years* below: Note 100.

87. Tarík Karenga, *The Pharaohs' 5 Laws of Success*, First Edition, (Union City: Amenism, Inc., 2022), 17, 20. *See* the term *spiritual rebirth*, in Tarík Karenga, *Review of the Kemetan Mystery System*, First Edition, (Union City: Amenism, Inc., in press).

88. Maulana Karenga, *Maat: The Moral Ideal in Ancient Egypt*, (Los Angeles: University of Sankore Press, 2006), 347. Tarík Karenga, *The Pharaohs' 5 Laws of Success*, First Edition, (Union City: Amenism, Inc., 2022), 1-2, 34. The writing system of Kemet is called "Medu Netur (**MEH**-doo nay-**TOOR**), meaning "*Words of God*." *Ibid.*, 11. The language of Kemet is called "Kemetan," and the three scripts used to <u>write</u> the language of Kemet are called *formal* Kemetan (also referred to as hieroglyphic), *hieratic*, and *demotic*. *See* the terms *Kemetan* and *Medu Netur* in Tarík Karenga, *Review of the Kemetan Mystery System*, First Edition, (Union City: Amenism, Inc., in press). Important note: One can become a man without ever having reached manhood.

89. Tarík Karenga, *The Pharaohs' 5 Laws of Success*, First Edition, (Union City: Amenism, Inc., 2022), 19. *See* the term *works of his father*, in Tarík Karenga, *Review of the Kemetan Mystery System*, First Edition, (Union City: Amenism, Inc., in press). *See also* D. M. Murdock, *Christ in Egypt: The Horus-Jesus Connection*, (Seattle: Stellar House Publishing, 2009), 417-419. Gerald Massey, *Ancient Egypt: The Light of the World*, Volume II, (London: T. Fisher Unwin, 1907), 796.

Near the beginning of this publication we learned that the birthday of Heru (as an Elder) is officially observed on the second day of the **calendrical five-day period** of Oup Renpet, which in turn corresponds to and falls on the <u>day</u> of the summer solstice, and therefore the particular type of eldership with which Heru is associated here is in reference to his preexistence as a living soul ahead of his biological birth in a physical body.[90] Here, Heru is styled *Heru-ur em Mehit* or Heru (as an Elder) in the <u>North</u>.[91] The above is in sharp contrast to the second type of eldership with which Heru is also associated and that pertains to his reaching a peak stage of development in biological life as the third person of the Holy Trinity; this, after having been born "feeble and weak" during the period of the winter solstice and in the season of Akhet (ah-**KET**) *i.e.*, the season of sowing, also known as winter. Here, Heru is styled *Heru-ur em Res* or Heru (as an Elder) in the <u>South</u>.[92]

Be acutely aware that ". . . the king is both human and divine and therefore as the mortal king his heavenly Father is Amen from whom his spirit was **begotten**, but because Ra gave **birth** to his soul he is, as a living soul, the 'Son of the Sun,' meaning the Son of Ra. Accordingly, as the third person of the Holy Trinity Heru, his divine father is Osir."[93]

**Stage 4:** The resurrection of the soul, its departure from its fallen human host, and its passage from the physical realm into the realm of spirit. The Litany of Ra says of the Pharaoh:

*". . . his spirit soars into the heavens, it rests there; his body descends to the earth . . ."*[94]

Amenism teaches that "it was not until after the birth of Heru and the subsequent defeat of Seth

---

*See* the term *heir* in Webster's New World Dictionary & Thesaurus, Version 2.0, Build #25, Accent Software International, Macmillan Publishers, 1998.

90. A similar mystery pertaining instead to Osir is found in an inscription taken from the south side base of the great obelisk of Karnak that records Pharaoh Queen Hatshepsut as having said of herself: "Horus (*i.e.*, Heru) the avenger of her father (*i.e.*, Osir), the elder of his mother's (*i.e.*, Nyut's (**NYOOT'S**)) husband (*i.e.*, Geb), whom [*sic*] Ra hath engendered to produce a glorious seed upon earth . . ." *i.e.*, Ra brought forth Osir by way of Nyut and Geb in order to produce Heru. P. Le Page Renouf, "Inscription of Queen Hatasu on the Base of the Great Obelisk of Karnak," in *Records of the Past*, Volume XII, Egyptian Texts, ed. Samuel Birch, (London: Samuel Bagster and Sons, 1874), 131. Mine in parentheses. Before Osir, the eldest of the five and firstborn came into being, he existed in Ñun. *See* above.

91. E. A. Wallis Budge, *The Gods of the Egyptians: Or, Studies in Egyptian Mythology*, Volume I, (London: Methuen & Company, 1904), 467-468. E. A. Wallis Budge, *An Egyptian Hieroglyphic Dictionary: In Two Volumes*, Volume I, (London: John Murray, 1920), 318a. W. E. Crum, *A Coptic Dictionary*, (New York: Oxford University Press, 1939), 212a.

92. E. A. Wallis Budge, *The Gods of the Egyptians: Or, Studies in Egyptian Mythology*, Volume I, (London: Methuen & Company, 1904), 467-468. E. A. Wallis Budge, *An Egyptian Hieroglyphic Dictionary: In Two Volumes*, Volume I, (London: John Murray, 1920), 431b. W. E. Crum, *A Coptic Dictionary*, (New York: Oxford University Press, 1939), 299b. D. M. Murdock, *Christ in Egypt: The Horus-Jesus Connection*, (Seattle: Stellar House Publishing, 2009), 111. Tarík Karenga, *The Pharaohs' 5 Laws of Success*, First Edition, (Union City: Amenism, Inc., 2022), 19. E. A. Wallis Budge, *Facsimiles of Egyptian Hieratic Papyri in the British Museum*, Series 1, (London: Oxford University Press, 1910), xvi. *See also*, E. A. Wallis Budge, *An Egyptian Hieroglyphic Dictionary: In Two Volumes*, Volume I, (London: John Murray, 1920), 8b.

93. Tarík Karenga, *The Pharaohs' 5 Laws of Success*, First Edition, (Union City: Amenism, Inc., 2022), 20. *See* the term *spiritual rebirth*, in Tarík Karenga, *Review of the Kemetan Mystery System*, First Edition, (Union City: Amenism, Inc., in press).

94. Edouard Naville, "The Litany of Ra," in *Records of the Past*, Volume VIII, Egyptian Texts, ed. Samuel Birch, (London: Samuel Bagster and Sons, 1874), 128. Italics mine.

that, with the assistance of Tekhi, her son Heru (as an Elder), and Anup (ah-**NOOP**), the Jackal-headed form of Amen, Iset resurrected her mummified husband Osir forthwith, whereas her son Heru (as an Elder) awakened him and raised him to his feet," and this is spoken of in the Mysteries as being brought out of *spiritual slumber*.[95] What next occurred was the ascension of Osir ". . . back to his kingdom in heaven as ruler and judge of the souls of those who have passed, leaving his son Heru to rule over his kingdom on earth," which from the perspective of the Pharaoh meant that he was carrying on in the traditions of his predecessors in general, and from the perspective of Heru, it meant that he was continuing the *works of his father* in particular (*see* Table 8).[96]

In the Mysteries this otherwise peripherally understood theological concept (*e.g.*, *spiritual resurrection*) is explained in this way. Every <u>new</u> king is literally Heru, the third person and Son of God on earth; however, upon the death and resurrection proper of the king, and provided that at judgment the king's heart is found to be righteous from having done *Maat* on earth, he is completely assimilated to Osir in the afterlife.[97] So from the perspective of the <u>new</u> king, he was carrying on in the traditions of his predecessors, but as the very person of Heru, he was continuing the *works of his father*.[98] That is why in the Mysteries *spiritual resurrection*, which is during one's biological life, results ". . . in renewed activity of the Ba (*i.e.*, soul) with regard to its being engaged for the practical purpose of transmitting civilization to all nations, which is the transference to earth of the Kingdom of Heaven located within one's own spirit."[99]

As for the resurrection of Osir, although he had been spiritually revived, Osir had also up until now been lying in an inactive state; and as for the resurrection proper of the deceased and <u>*former*</u> Pharaoh, who thereafter ascended to heaven and was completely assimilated <u>to</u> Osir, both events, which are seen also as the resurrection of the Sun *i.e.*, the soul, are officially observed on the morning of the thirtieth day of the month of Paen Rennñutet (**PAH**-en ren-**NYOO**-tet) or March 21st (Gregorian) during the season of Pert (**PERT**) *i.e.*, during the season of growing and harvesting, exactly **three days after** both Osir and the deceased and <u>*former*</u> Pharaoh were placed in their respective tombs, and what is more, this

---

95. Tarík Karenga, *The Pharaohs' 5 Laws of Success*, First Edition, (Union City: Amenism, Inc., 2022), 17. Heru gives his own restored eye to his father Osir to assist in his resurrection. E. A. Wallis Budge, *Osiris and the Egyptian Resurrection*, Volume I, (New York: G. P. Putnam's Sons, 1911), 82-86. *See* the term *spiritual slumber*, in Tarík Karenga, *Review of the Kemetan Mystery System*, First Edition, (Union City: Amenism, Inc., in press).

96. Tarík Karenga, *The Pharaohs' 5 Laws of Success*, First Edition, (Union City: Amenism, Inc., 2022), 18. *See* the term *works of his father*, in Tarík Karenga, *Review of the Kemetan Mystery System*, First Edition, (Union City: Amenism, Inc., in press). *See also* D. M. Murdock, *Christ in Egypt: The Horus-Jesus Connection*, (Seattle: Stellar House Publishing, 2009), 417-419.

97. Tarík Karenga, *The Pharaohs' 5 Laws of Success*, First Edition, (Union City: Amenism, Inc., 2022), 21, 54.

98. Tarík Karenga, *The Pharaohs' 5 Laws of Success*, First Edition, (Union City: Amenism, Inc., 2022), 19, 21. *See* the term *works of his father*, in Tarík Karenga, *Review of the Kemetan Mystery System*, First Edition, (Union City: Amenism, Inc., in press). *See also* D. M. Murdock, *Christ in Egypt: The Horus-Jesus Connection*, (Seattle: Stellar House Publishing, 2009), 417-419.

99. Tarík Karenga, *The Pharaohs' 5 Laws of Success*, First Edition, (Union City: Amenism, Inc., 2022), 21. Mine in parentheses. *See* the terms *spiritual resurrection* and *works of his father*, in Tarík Karenga, *Review of the Kemetan Mystery System*, First Edition, (Union City: Amenism, Inc., in press).

is the same day on which the Sun enters the zodiacal sign Aries *i.e.*, the sign of the Ram (a <u>mature</u> male sheep), which is significant in view of the fact that on the following day, that is, on the first day of the month of Paen Khonsu or March 22nd (Gregorian), the *new* king ascended the throne and the ancient Kemetans ". . . celebrated this season by sacrificing a lamb" *i.e.*, a <u>young</u> sheep which they identified with Heru (as a child), so as to symbolically represent the self-sacrificial transformation or crossing over from that early stage of development when the Pharaoh, as the very person of Heru, was spiritually immature, but who clearly was now an Elder and spiritually equipped; and thus, all of the above corresponds to the astronomical event of the spring (*i.e.*, vernal) equinox when ". . . the Sun crosses the celestial equator moving north," marking the point at which "night and day are of equal length," and beginning "a period in which the hours of light exceed the hours of darkness" (*see* Plates 1 and 3).[100]

With this in mind, **"Three days later"** on the fourth day of the month of Paen Khonsu or March 25th (Gregorian), the ancient Kemetans, "celebrated the (*spiritual*) resurrection of the young sun god" *i.e.*, the *new* king and person of Heru, who henceforth began to carry on in the traditions of his predecessors, and to continue the *works of his father* Osir (*see* Plate 1).[101]

---

100. James Bonwick, *Egyptian Belief and Modern Thought*, (London: C. Kegan Paul & Co., 1878), 155. Ernest Busenbark, *Symbols, Sex, and the Stars in Popular Beliefs*, (New York: The Truth Seeker Company, Inc., 1949), 20, (119), 120, 149. Godfrey Higgins, *Anacalypsis*, Volume II, (London: Longman, Rees, Orme, Brown, Green, and Longman Paternoster Row, 1836), 102. H. W. Fairman, "Worship and Festivals in an Egyptian Temple," *Bulletin of the John Rylands Library* 37, no. 1 (1954): 192. Alan H. Gardiner, "Reviewed Work(s): The Golden Bough: Adonis, Attis, Osiris; Studies in the History of Oriental Religion by J. G. Frazer," *The Journal of Egyptian Archaeology* 2, no. 2 (1915): 123-125. Eric Chaisson and Steve McMillan, *Astronomy: A Beginner's Guide to the Universe*, Fifth Edition, (Upper Saddle River: Pearson Prentice Hall, 2007), 11. D. M. Murdock, *Christ in Egypt: The Horus-Jesus Connection*, (Seattle: Stellar House Publishing, 2009), 83, 383, 390, 516. E. A. Wallis Budge, *Facsimiles of Egyptian Hieratic Papyri in the British Museum*, Series 1, (London: Oxford University Press, 1910), xvi. E. A. Wallis Budge, *An Egyptian Hieroglyphic Dictionary: In Two Volumes*, Volume I, (London: John Murray, 1920), 242b. *See* also "equinox" in Webster's New World Dictionary & Thesaurus, Version 2.0, Build #25, Accent Software International, Macmillan Publishers, 1998. Dates are according to the Kemetan calendar. According to Amenism, Osir was entombed at **twelve o'clock midnight** on the twenty-sixth day of the month of Paen Renñutet, and was raised from the dead exactly three days later, which is interpreted also as **twelve o'clock in the morning** on the thirtieth day of that same month. It is <u>incorrect</u> to say that Heru was symbolically crucified at the spring equinox, because *spiritual crucifixion* occurs only upon the entrance of the soul into a human host and is instead associated with the fall equinox. Murdock, *op. cit.*, 2009, 359, 362-364. Heru is the sacrificial "Lamb of God." *Ibid.*, 331-332. Higgins, Volume II, *op. cit.*, 1836, 107-112. Logan Mitchell, *Religion in the Heavens; Or, Mythology Unveiled*, (London: Freethought Publishing Company, 1881), 94-95. Plagiarized, adapted and reconfigured versions of these Amenist teachings (*e.g.*, the *missing years*, the sacrificial *lamb of God*, and *revival* followed by the *resurrection*) are in the religion of Christianity. *See* The Holy Bible: *Comprising the Old and New Testaments*, The King James Version, (New York: American Bible Society, 1972), [(OT) Hosea 6:2], 808; [(NT) Matthew 12:40, 26:61], 13, 31; [Mark 8:31], 44; [Luke 3:23], 61; [John 1:29, 36, 2:19], 94, 95, 96. In the Mysteries it is said that the deceased Pharaoh is embalmed before he joins Ra, who we have learned is Osir. *See* Eric Orlin, ed., *The Routledge Encyclopedia of Ancient Mediterranean Religions*, (New York: Routledge, 2016), 103. *See* also the terms *spiritual rebirth* and *spiritual resurrection* in Tarík Karenga, *Review of the Kemetan Mystery System*, First Edition, (Union City: Amenism, Inc., in press). Important note: the closing events of the reenactment of the passion play of Osir during the month of Ka Hera Ka (Khoiak in Coptic) extended into the first day of the following month of Ta Aobyti (Tybi in Coptic) with the *dramatized* accession of the *new* king, while the actual accession of the *new* king took place on the first day of the month of Paen Khonsu. *See* Gerald Massey, *Ancient Egypt: The Light of the World*, Volume II, (London: T. Fisher Unwin, 1907), 740. *See* also Plate 1 below.

101. Ernest Busenbark, *Symbols, Sex, and the Stars in Popular Beliefs*, (New York: The Truth Seeker Company, Inc., 1949), 119. Mine in bold. Mine in parentheses. Often mistakenly transposed are the dates of the resurrection proper

Finally, Egyptologist E. A. Wallis Budge informs us that: "The central point of each Osirian's Religion was his hope of resurrection in a transformed body and of immortality, which could only be realized by him through the (life,) death and resurrection of [[Osir]]."[102] Hence, this section along with the chapter appropriately concludes with an ancient Kemetan passing ceremony for the living souls of those whose human host has fallen titled: "*Thess em Hotep*," meaning "Rise Up in Peace" (R.U.I.P.):[103]

*"O you, who bring beneficent souls into the house of (the Christ) and risen savior Osir, bring this excellent soul with you, our sister/brother [INSERT NAME OF THE DEPARTED]; let her/him see as you see, let her/him hear as you hear, let her/him stand up even as you stand up and sit down as you sit down.*

*O you who give bread and beer to beneficent souls in the house of Osir, give bread and beer day and night to this soul whose words are true before God, our sister/brother [INSERT NAME OF THE DEPARTED].*

*O you who open the way and clear the path for beneficent souls, open the way and clear the path for this soul [INSERT NAME OF THE DEPARTED] whose voice is vindicated.*

*May she/he enter in boldness and come forth in peace from the house of Osir, may she/he not be opposed or turned back, may she/he enter paradise praised and come forth loved and triumphant; may her/his words travel with you, may she/he not be found deficient in the balance and be free from all fault.*

*May she/he not be judged according to the mouth of the multitude that do not know her/him, but may her/his soul be lifted up itself before her/his heart and be found to be righteous on earth.*

*May she/he come into the presence of the Lord of Lords, may she/he reach the Hall of Righteousness, may she/he rise like a living goddess/god and give forth light like the divine powers that are in heaven; may she/he proceed in peace.*

---

of Osir and the *spiritual resurrection* of the <u>new</u> king, who although during biological life ruled as Heru, he nevertheless occupied the throne by virtue of his identification with Osir, and like his predecessors, he too was, in the afterlife, completely assimilated to him. *See* Godfrey Higgins, *Anacalypsis*, Volume II, (London: Longman, Rees, Orme, Brown, Green, and Longman Paternoster Row, 1836), 102. *See* also "Stage 3" above. Resurrection proper is experienced after one's biological death and is in sharp contrast to *spiritual resurrection*, which is experienced during one's biological life. *See* the term *spiritual resurrection*, in Tarík Karenga, *Review of the Kemetan Mystery System*, First Edition, (Union City: Amenism, Inc., in press). Important note: Dates are according to the Kemetan calendar. A plagiarized, adapted and reconfigured version of this Amenist teaching is in the religion of Christianity. *See* The Holy Bible: *Comprising the Old and New Testaments*, The King James Version, (New York: American Bible Society, 1972), [(NT) Matthew 12:40, 26:61], 13, 31; [Mark 8:31], 44; [John 2:19], 96.

102. Tarík Karenga, *The Pharaohs' 5 Laws of Success*, First Edition, (Union City: Amenism, Inc., 2022), 90-91.

103. Maulana Karenga, *Kwanzaa & the Dialog with African Culture: Recovery and Reaffirmation* [Audio Presentation], Us Organization, 1995. *See* also E. A. Wallis Budge, *An Egyptian Hieroglyphic Dictionary: In Two Volumes*, Volume I, (London: John Murray, 1920), 264a, 517b. *See* also E. A. Wallis Budge, *An Egyptian Hieroglyphic Dictionary: In Two Volumes*, Volume II, (London: John Murray, 1920), 861a. *See* the terms *biological death* and *second death*, in Tarík Karenga, *Review of the Kemetan Mystery System*, First Edition, (Union City: Amenism, Inc., in press).

*May the Lords of the sacred land receive her/him and give her/him three-fold praise in peace, may they make a seat for her/him on the council of the elders; may she/he ascend in the presence of the Beneficent One and may she/he assume whatever form she/he wants in whatever place her/his spirit wishes to be.*

*And may she/he be given this promise: a spirit in heaven, a continuing power on earth, justification in God's domain and resurrection even after death. These are the gifts of the righteous person and a righteous person is she/he who receives them. She/he shall be counted among the ancestors, her/his name shall endure as a monument and what she/he has done on earth shall never perish nor pass away."*[104] *[INSERT NAME OF DEPARTED]–thess em hotep, rise up in peace.*

---

104. The reading is a conflation of several variant renderings of the passing ceremony from the religion of Amenism and as such, slight modifications have been made. For example, the spelling of the name "Osir," which refers to the first person of God Ra, is consistent with the teachings of Amenism and has therefore been substituted for the name "Osiris," which is Greek. Mine in parentheses and brackets. *See* Maulana Karenga, *Kwanzaa & the Dialog with African Culture: Recovery and Reaffirmation* [Audio Presentation], Us Organization, 1995. Maulana Karenga, *Selections from the Husia*, (Los Angeles: University Of Sankore Press, 1984), 105-106. Maulana Karenga, *The Book of Coming Forth by Day: The Ethics of the Declarations of Innocence*, (Los Angeles: University of Sankore Press, 1990), 36-37. *See* also Sir P. Le Page Renouf and Prof. E. Naville, *The Egyptian Book of the Dead: Translation and Commentary*, (London: The Society of Biblical Archaeology, 1904), 2. *See* also E. A. Wallis Budge, *The Book of the Dead: The Papyrus of Ani in the British Museum*, (London: Kegan Paul, Trench, Trubner & Co., 1895), 22-24. E. A. Wallis Budge, *The Book of the Dead: The Papyrus of Ani*, In Two Volumes, Volume II, (London: The Medici Society, Ltd., 1913), 360-365. Osir is the Christ and risen savior; *see* Tarík Karenga, *The Pharaohs' 5 Laws of Success*, First Edition, (Union City: Amenism, Inc., 2022), 23-25.

CHAPTER TWO

# THE ZODIAC

Twelve signs or star constellations constitute the Zodiac **through which the Sun passes** annually as it appears to travel through the sky along the ecliptic (*i.e.*, "... the plane of Earth's orbit around the Sun"), and **as viewed from earth**, each of these twelve signs are visible in the night sky annually in the following order: Pisces, Aries, Taurus, Gemini, Kheper, Leo, Virgo, Libra, Scorpio, Sagittarius, Capricorn and Aquarius.[1] There is also; however, a **precessional path** of the Sun through the signs of the Zodiac in reverse order to that of the annual path; for example, 1) Aquarius, 2) Capricorn, 3) Sagittarius, 4) Scorpio, 5) Libra, 6) Virgo, 7) Leo, 8) Kheper, 9) Gemini, 10) Taurus, 11) Aries, and 12) Pisces (*see* Plate 3).[2]

To illustrate, the spring equinox **on which the Sun rises once annually** and which "... is defined in astronomy as that point in space where the plane of the Earth's orbit around the Sun, the ecliptic, intersects the plane of the Earth's equator extended into space," falls backward through the signs of the Zodiac due to the wobbling movement of the earth as it spins on its axis known as **precession**, and this phenomenon has the observable effect of advancing the constellations forward past the above equinoctial point at the rate of about one degree, or one day, every 72 years.[3] Hence, the period of time that elapses from the moment that any one particular sign of the Zodiac reaches and then advances past the spring equinox is called a **zodiacal Age**, whereas the period of time that comprises all twelve zodiacal Ages is called the **"Great Year."**[4] It is therefore important to understand that "... the signs of the Zodiac are

---

1. Frances Sakoian and Louis S. Acker, *The Astrologer's Handbook*, (New York: Collins Reference, 1973), 3. *See* also Michael E. Bakich, *The Cambridge Guide to the Constellations*, (New York: Cambridge University Press, 1995), 62-64. The **annual path** of the Sun through the signs of the Zodiac beginning with the zodiacal sign Pisces is according to Amenism. The **precessional path** of the Sun through the signs of the Zodiac therefore begins with the zodiacal sign Aquarius, the Water Bearer, and from water the remaining signs emerge.

2. Thomas G. Brophy, *The Origin Map: Discovery of a Prehistoric, Megalithic, Astrophysical Map and Sculpture of the Universe*, (New York: Writers Club Press, 2002), xix. The reverse numerical order of the signs of the Zodiac is according to Amenism and is based on the **precessional path** of the Sun through the signs of the Zodiac.

3. Frances Sakoian and Louis S. Acker, *The Astrologer's Handbook*, (New York: Collins Reference, 1973), 3. *See* also Sidney G. P. Coryn, *The Faith of Ancient Egypt*, (New York: Theosophical Publishing Company, 1913), 13-14, 39. *See* also, George St. Clair, *Creation Records Discovered in Egypt: Studies in the Book of the Dead*, (London: David Nutt, 1898), 43. *See* also Jay M. Pasachoff, Astronomy: *From the Earth to the Universe*, Third Edition, (New York: Saunders College Publishing, 1987), 98. *See* also Thomas G. Brophy, *The Origin Map: Discovery of a Prehistoric, Megalithic, Astrophysical Map and Sculpture of the Universe*, (New York: Writers Club Press, 2002), xix.

4. E. A. Wallis Budge, *A History of Egypt*, Volume I, (London: Kegan Paul, Trench, Trubner & Co., Ltd., 1902), 163. *See* also Thomas G. Brophy, *The Origin Map: Discovery of a Prehistoric, Megalithic, Astrophysical Map and Sculpture of the Universe*, (New York: Writers Club Press, 2002), xix.

defined by the Earth's yearly revolution around the Sun," but their reverse numerical order as well as the zodiacal Ages are defined by precession (*see* Table 6).[5]

| Table 6: Kemetan Zodiac Data — Sign | "Sun in" "Soul in" Dates | Number of Days | Length of Zodiacal Age | Visibility Midnight Culmination[6] |
|---|---|---|---|---|
| 1. Aquarius | 1 Ap Ap – 1 Oup Renpet<br><br>21 May – 20 June | 31 | 31 x 72 = **2,232 years** | 2 Aope<br><br>25 Aug |
| 2. Capricorn | 2 Oup Renpet – 28 Mesut Ra<br><br>21 June – 22 July | 32 | 32 x 72 = **2,304 years** | 15 Tekh<br><br>8 Aug |
| 3. Sagittarius | 29 Mesut Ra – 29 Tekhi<br><br>23 July – 22 August | 31 | 31 x 72 = **2,232 years** | 13 Mesu<br><br>7 Jul |
| 4. Scorpio | 30 Tekhi – 30 Paen Aopet<br><br>23 August – 22 September | 31 | 31 x 72 = **2,232 years** | 14 Ap Ap<br><br>3 Jun |
| 5. Libra | 1 Het-Heru – 30 Het-Heru<br><br>23 September – 22 October | 30 | 30 x 72 = **2,160 years** | 19 Ayni<br><br>9 May |
| 6. Virgo | 1 Ka Hera Ka – 30 Ka Hera Ka<br><br>23 October – 21 November | 30 | 30 x 72 = **2,160 years** | 21 Khon<br><br>11 Apr |
| 7. Leo | 1 Ta Aobyti – 30 Ta Aobyti<br><br>22 November – 21 December | 30 | 30 x 72 = **2,160 years** | 10 Renñ<br><br>1 Mar |
| 8. Kheper | 1 Makhiar – 29 Makhiar<br><br>22 December – 19 January | 29 | 29 x 72 = **2,088 years** | 10 Amen*<br><br>30 Jan |
| 9. Gemini | 30 Makhiar – 29 Paen Amenhotep<br><br>20 January – 18 February | 30 | 30 x 72 = **2,160 years** | 15 Makh<br><br>5 Jan |
| 10 Taurus | 30 Paen Amenhotep – 29 Paen Renñutet<br><br>19 February – 20 March | 30 | 30 x 72 = **2,160 years** | 9 Aoby<br><br>30 Nov |
| 11. Aries | 30 Paen Renñutet – 29 Paen Khonsu<br><br>21 March – 19 April | 30 | 30 x 72 = **2,160 years** | 8 Ka<br><br>30 Oct |
| 12. Pisces | 30 Paen Khonsu – 30 Paen Aynit<br><br>20 April – 20 May | 31 | 31 x 72 = **2,232 years** | 5 Het-<br><br>27 Sep |

5. Frances Sakoian and Louis S. Acker, *The Astrologer's Handbook*, (New York: Collins Reference, 1973), 7. Note: According to Amenism.

6. Midnight culmination is ". . . the meridian passage of a constellation (more specifically, the *center* of the constellation) when the constellation lies 180° from the Sun . . . (i)t is, therefore, the best night of the year to view a particular constellation, depending, of course, on the phase of the Moon." *See* Michael E. Bakich, *The Cambridge Guide to the Constellations*, (New York: Cambridge University Press, 1995), 8, 62-64. * Non leap year date.

Based on the information provided above, the length of the Great Year; therefore, equals **26, 280 years**, and because the Sepdtaic cycle consisting of **1,460 years**, the calendrical cycle consisting of **365 days** and the practical circle consisting of **360 degrees** all divide evenly into the zodiacal cycle consisting of **26,280 years** which constitutes the Great Year, the resultant harmonious configuration between the zodiacal cycle and that of the Sepdtaic, that of the calendrical, and that of the practical is expressed as a circle inside of a circle, inside of a circle, inside of a circle.[7] Now, couple with these facts that ancient Greek legislator Solon traveled to Kemet in 590 B.C.E. (and possibly a second time in 561 B.C.E.) where he was told by a Kemetan priest that Kemet ". . . possessed the stored wisdom of 50,000 years," and we shall see the truth in the Amenist teaching that Kemetan history began in the year 0 or 50561 B.C.E. followed by the first day of the first month of the Kemetan calendar year 1 or 50560 B.C.E. at the beginning of the Age of Aquarius, as if to allude to our civilization as having emerged from the primordial waters of Ñun at Zep Tepi, such as we are now experiencing with its reemergence of recent times, and with its inevitably being reconnected with the rest of Africa (*see* Table 7).[8]

**Table 7: Chronological Table[9]**

| Kemetan | Gregorian | Events | Comments |
|---|---|---|---|
| 52582 | 2022 | The Revocation of the Edicts of Theodosius and Justinian. | Kemetan temples officially reopened |
| 52580 | 2020 | The Reemergent Kingdom<br>**Kemet emerges for the second time as the Kingdom of God on earth.** | **34th Dynasty**<br>Founder: Tarík Karenga |
| 52579 | 2019 | President of the West African nation of Ghana, Nana Akufo-Addo, declares the year 2019 C.E. the "Year of Return . . . giving fresh impetus to the quest to unite Africans on the continent with their brothers and sisters in the Diaspora" and commemorating 400 years since enslaved Africans arrived in Virginia in 1619 (Tetteh, Dec. 2018 – Mar. 2019). | African nations and societies beginning to collectively restore themselves and reproject their own priorities |

7. Cheikh Anta Diop, *Civilization or Barbarism: An Authentic Anthropology*, (Brooklyn: Lawrence Hill Books, 1991), 344.

8. Sidney G. P. Coryn, *The Faith of Ancient Egypt*, (New York: Theosophical Publishing Company, 1913), 10. *See* also Diogenes Laertius, *The Lives and Opinions of Eminent Philosophers*, Translated by C. D. Yonge, (London: George Bell and Sons, 1901), 25. Cheikh Anta Diop, *Civilization or Barbarism: An Authentic Anthropology*, (Brooklyn: Lawrence Hill Books, 1991), 84. *See* also George Rawlinson, *History of Herodotus*, In Four Volumes, Volume 1, (London: John Murray, 1862), 138 (note 8), 139. "The history of Black Africa will remain suspended in the air and cannot be written correctly until African historians dare to connect it with the history of Egypt." Cheikh Anta Diop, *The African Origin of Civilization: Myth or Reality*, (Chicago: Lawrence Hill Books, 1974), xiv. Note: According to Amenism, the first day beginning at the end of the five-day summer solstice period (*e.g.*, June 25th) when the Sun ". . . reverses its movement and **begins to *visibly* rise increasingly southward . . .**" marks the beginning of the Kemetan calendar year. *See* "Stage 1" above.

9. Adapted from the chronological table in Cheikh Anta Diop, *Civilization or Barbarism: An Authentic Anthropology*, (Brooklyn: Lawrence Hill Books, 1991), 23.

| | | | |
|---|---|---|---|
| Makh. 52569 | Jan. 2009 | First African American (*i.e.*, black) Man and Woman serve as President and First Lady of the United States of America, the same nation that had previously engaged in the mass kidnapping, enslavement, rape, torture, and murder of Africans from *circa* 1400 to 1865 C.E. | Barack and Michelle Obama (8 years in office) |
| 52561 | 2000 | Second full revolution of the Zodiac since Zep Tepi; New Year's Day; Age of Aquarius begins; Heliacal rising of Sepdta on Tekhi 16th. | **Great Year 3** Sahu begins to descend from its precessional northern culmination. \*\*\* |
| 52426 | 1865 | Holocaust of Enslavement period ends | End of the Civil War |
| c. 51961 | c. 1400 | Holocaust of Enslavement period begins | More African societies in decline |
| 51201 | 640 | Arabs arrive in Kemet Around this same time, the last of six migratory waves leaves Kemet; **Official end date of first emergence of Kemet as the Kingdom of God on earth.** | Conversion to the religion of Islam |
| 51101 | 540 | Heliacal rising of Sepdta on Tekhi 16th | |
| 51090 | 529 | Edict of Justinian | Last Kemetan temples and universities closed |
| 50941 | 380 | Edict of Theodosius | Ordered the closing of Kemetan temples |
| 50562 | 1 | | Standard calculations for Gregorian dates utilize the year 0 |
| 50561 | 0 | [Synchronization] | |
| 50560 | -1 | | |
| 50531-51200 | -30 to 640 | Roman conquest of Kemet | Beginning of the adoption of Christianity |
| 50329 | -232 | Age of Pisces begins | |
| 50256-50531 | -305 to -30 | The Ptolemies | **33rd Dynasty** Founder: Ptolemy I |
| 50229-50256 | -332 to -305 | Greek conquest of Kemet | **32nd Dynasty** Founder: Alexander III |

| | | | |
|---|---|---|---|
| 50218-50229 | -343 to -332 | "Second period of Persian occupation" (Van De Mieroop, 2011, p. 290). | **31st Dynasty** Founder: Artaxerxes III |
| 50036-50157 | -525 to -404 | Persian conquest of Kemet<br><br>First of six migratory waves leaves Kemet and eventually reaches West Africa. | **27th Dynasty** Founder: Cambyses II |
| 50000 | -561 | Greek legislator Solon possibly travels to Kemet a second time where he is informed by a Kemetan priest that Kemetan history spans 50,000 years.<br><br>"And what happened on the latter occasion may have been transferred to the former" (Rawlinson, Volume 1, 1862, p. 138 (note 8)). | Herodotus: Book I<br><br>Amenism is therefore the oldest religion in the world. |
| 49971 | -590 | Greek legislator Solon travels to Kemet. | Town of Sais |
| c. 49898-50036 | c. -663 to -525 | Assyrian conquest of Kemet | **26th Dynasty** Founder: Psammetichus |
| c. 49851 | c. -710 | Memphite Theology or *Shabaka Text* copied and preserved during the 25th Dynasty. | ". . . earliest record of creation described as an act of creative thought and speech" (Karenga, 1993, p. 82). |
| c. 49805-49905 | c. -756 to -656 | Ta-Setian (*i.e.*, ancient Sudanese) conquest of Kemet | **25th Dynasty** Founder: Piankhi |
| 49641 | -920 | Heliacal rising of Sepdta on Tekhi 16th | |
| c. 49616-49846 | c. -945 to -715 | Libyan conquest of Kemet | **22nd Dynasty** Founder: Sheshonk I |
| c. 49476-50229 | c. -1085 to -332 | The Late Period Priest-Kings rule Kemet until c. -945 | **21st Dynasty** Founder: Her-Heru |
| c. 48994-49476 | c. -1567 to -1085 | The New Kingdom | **18th Dynasty** Founder: Aahmes I |
| c. 48775-48994 | c. -1786 to -1567 | The Second Intermediate Period | **13th Dynasty** Founder: Ra-Khu-Taui |
| c. 48521-48776 | c. -2040 to -1785 | Coffin Texts or *Book of Vindication* | Sacred texts inscribed on the inside walls of coffins; Middle Kingdom |

| | | | |
|---|---|---|---|
| c. 48511-48775 | c. -2050 to -1786 | The Middle Kingdom | **11th Dynasty** Founder: Ñyntef I |
| c. 48421 | c. -2140 | Book of Kheti | ". . . earliest known concept of humans as the images of God" (Karenga, 2006, p. 318). |
| c. 48380-48511 | c. -2181 to -2050 | The First Intermediate Period | **7th Dynasty** Founder: Nefer-Ka |
| c. 48211-48251 | c. -2350 to -2310 | Book of Ptah Hotep; ". . . vizier or prime minister of King Isesi of the Fifth Dynasty" (Karenga, 2006, p. 35). | Oldest known complete wisdom book |
| 48181 | -2380 | Heliacal rising of Sepdta on Tekhi 16th | |
| 48169 | -2392 | Age of Aries begins | |
| c. 48161-48261 | c. -2400 to -2300 | Pyramid Texts of King Unas of the 5th Dynasty. | Beginning of the practice of adorning the interior walls of pyramids with sacred texts |
| c. 47875-48379 | c. -2686 to -2182 | The Old Kingdom | **3rd Dynasty** Founder: Djoser |
| c. 47261-47875 | c. -3300** to -2686 | The Early Dynastic Period  Kemet united into one kingdom. | **1st Dynasty** Founder: Mena |
| c. 47044-47261 | c. -3517 to -3300 | The Transition Period Kemet as the Kingdom of God on earth is *ruled by eight "Demi-Gods"* (Budge, 1902, pp. 163, 179); *see* also (Diop, 1974, p. 140).  Kemet divided into two kingdoms. | 217 year reign  The "Shemsu Heru" *i.e.,* the Followers of Heru (Budge, 1902, p. 165). |
| c. 46761 | c. -3800 | Ta-Setian (*i.e.,* ancient Sudanese) Pharaonic civilization | Predating the uniting of Kemet by King Mena |
| 46721 | -3840 | Heliacal rising of Sepdta on Tekhi 16th | |
| 46325 | -4236* | Kemetan ". . . Astronomical calendar already in use" (Diop, 1991, p. 23). | |
| 46009 | -4552 | Age of Taurus begins | |
| 45261 | -5300 | Heliacal rising of Sepdta on Tekhi 16th | |

| | | | |
|---|---|---|---|
| 43849 | -6712 | Age of Gemini begins | |
| 43801 | -6760 | Heliacal rising of Sepdta on Tekhi 16th | |
| c. 43561-47044 | c. -7000 to -3517 | The Inaugural Kingdom<br>**Kemet emerges for the first time as the Kingdom of God on earth** and is *ruled by Osir*, as he is one of the Twelve Gods; also, Kemet, meaning the *Black Community of Christ*, is also "a secret order comprising native African votaries of Christ (Osir)" (Karenga, 2022, p. 25, 41).<br>A Kingdom on earth now exists simultaneously with a Kingdom in Heaven. Kemetans transition to ". . . a pastoral and agricultural life" (Bakr, 1981, p. 84). The remaining gods rule in turn.<br><br>". . . by 7000 B.C., the Sahara had dried up" (Diop, 1974, p. 22). | In the Mysteries: "When Geb, his father, retired to the heavens, Osiris succeeded him as king of Egypt and took Isis, his sister, as queen" (Guirand, 1960, p. 16).<br><br>*"The Ethiopians say that the Egyptians are one of their colonies*, which was led into Egypt by Osiris" (Diop, 1982, p. 18). |
| c. 43060-47044 | c. -7501 to -3517 | Kemet as the Kingdom of Heaven within God's spirit that dwells in humans is *ruled by Geb* ". . . and the remaining gods, [all told] 12 in number" (Waddell, 1964, p. 229). | 3,984 year reign of the Twelve Gods: Osir, Iset, Heru, Nebt-Het, Seth, Het-Heru, Montu, Atum, Shu, Tefnyut, Geb, Nyut. |
| c. 42561 | c. -8000 | Kemet (the land) ". . . rose from the waters of the Nile and its lakes and marshes" (Karenga, 1993, p. 79). | Kemet was gradually built up by the topsoil carried down during the annual rains in the highlands of Abyssinia. |
| 42341 | -8220 | Heliacal rising of Sepdta on Tekhi 16th | |
| 41761 | -8800 | Age of Kheper begins | |
| 40881 | -9680 | Heliacal rising of Sepdta on Tekhi 16th | |
| 39601 | -10960 | Age of Leo begins | Sahu begins to ascend from its precessional southern culmination. *** |
| 39421 | -11140 | Heliacal rising of Sepdta on Tekhi 16th | |
| 37961 | -12600 | Heliacal rising of Sepdta on Tekhi 16th | |
| 37441 | -13120 | Age of Virgo begins | |
| 36501 | -14060 | Heliacal rising of Sepdta on Tekhi 16th | |

| | | | |
|---|---|---|---|
| 35281 | -15280 | Age of Libra begins | |
| 35041 | -15520 | Heliacal rising of Sepdta on Tekhi 16th | |
| 33581 | -16980 | Heliacal rising of Sepdta on Tekhi 16th | |
| 33049 | -17512 | Age of Scorpio begins | |
| 32121 | -18440 | Heliacal rising of Sepdta on Tekhi 16th | |
| 30817 | -19744 | Age of Sagittarius begins | |
| 30661 | -19900 | Heliacal rising of Sepdta on Tekhi 16th | |
| 29201 | -21360 | Heliacal rising of Sepdta on Tekhi 16th | |
| 28513 | -22048 | Age of Capricorn begins | |
| 27741 | -22820 | Heliacal rising of Sepdta on Tekhi 16th | |
| 26281 | -24280 | First full revolution of the Zodiac since Zep Tepi; New Year's Day; Age of Aquarius begins; Heliacal rising of Sepdta on Tekhi 16th. | **Great Year 2** Sahu begins to descend from its precessional northern culmination. *** |
| 24821 | -25740 | Heliacal rising of Sepdta on Tekhi 16th | |
| 24049 | -26512 | Age of Pisces begins | |
| 23361 | -27200 | Heliacal rising of Sepdta on Tekhi 16th | |
| 21901 | -28660 | Heliacal rising of Sepdta on Tekhi 16th | |
| 21889 | -28672 | Age of Aries begins | |
| 20441 | -30120 | Heliacal rising of Sepdta on Tekhi 16th | |
| 19729 | -30832 | Age of Taurus begins | |
| 18981 | -31580 | Heliacal rising of Sepdta on Tekhi 16th | |
| 17569 | -32992 | Age of Gemini begins | |
| 17521 | -33040 | Heliacal rising of Sepdta on Tekhi 16th | |
| 16061 | -34500 | Heliacal rising of Sepdta on Tekhi 16th | |
| 15481 | -35080 | Age of Kheper begins | |

| | | | |
|---|---|---|---|
| 14601 | -35960 | Heliacal rising of Sepdta on Tekhi 16th | |
| 13321 | -37240 | Age of Leo begins | Sahu begins to ascend from its precessional southern culmination. *** |
| 13141 | -37420 | Heliacal rising of Sepdta on Tekhi 16th | |
| c. 13060-43060 | c. -37501 to -7501 | Kemet as the Kingdom of Heaven within God's spirit that dwells in humans is *ruled by Ra*. | 30,000 year reign |
| 11681 | -38880 | Heliacal rising of Sepdta on Tekhi 16th | |
| 11161 | -39400 | Age of Virgo begins | |
| 10221 | -40340 | Heliacal rising of Sepdta on Tekhi 16th | |
| 9001 | -41560 | Age of Libra begins | |
| 8761 | -41800 | Heliacal rising of Sepdta on Tekhi 16th | |
| 7301 | -43260 | Heliacal rising of Sepdta on Tekhi 16th | |
| 6769 | -43792 | Age of Scorpio begins | |
| 5841 | -44720 | Heliacal rising of Sepdta on Tekhi 16th | |
| 4537 | -46024 | Age of Sagittarius begins | |
| 4381 | -46180 | Heliacal rising of Sepdta on Tekhi 16th | |
| 2921 | -47640 | Heliacal rising of Sepdta on Tekhi 16th | |
| 2233 | -48328 | Age of Capricorn begins | |
| 1461 | -49100 | Heliacal rising of Sepdta on Tekhi 16th | |
| 1 Z.T.E. | -50560 | **Zep Tepi**<br><br>Kemet established as the Kingdom of Heaven within God's spirit that dwells in humans and is *ruled by the Gods*, beginning with Ptah;<br><br>Age of Aquarius begins; Heliacal rising of Sepdta on Tekhi 16th. | **Great Year 1**<br><br>Abyssinia (*i.e.*, ancient Ethiopia); Ptah reigns approximately 13,059 years.<br><br>Sahu begins to descend from its precessional northern culmination. *** |
| **0** | -50561 | Beginning of Kemetan History; Amenism (oldest religion in the world according to Kemetan priests). | **0** symbolically represents Ñun (nonexistence). |

| | | | |
|---|---|---|---|
| 1 B.Z.T. | -50562 | Before Zep Tepi | |
| c. 99,439 B.Z.T. | c. -150,000 | First *Homo sapiens sapiens* | Omo Valley and Kanjera; Humans ". . . spread to all the then habitable parts of the Nile basin" (Diop, 1981, p. 66). |
| c. 5,449,439 B.Z.T. | c. -5,500,000 | Birth of humanity | East Africa's Great Lakes region |

*Source:* Amenism[10]

10. *See* also Cheikh Anta Diop, *Civilization or Barbarism: An Authentic Anthropology*, (Brooklyn: Lawrence Hill Books, 1991), xix, 11, 23, 33, 35, 53, 84, 148-149, 278-279*, 281**. Cheikh Anta Diop, *The African Origin of Civilization: Myth or Reality*, (Chicago: Lawrence Hill Books, 1974), 22, 88, 140, 146, 222. Cheikh Anta Diop, "Origin of the Ancient Egyptians," in *Journal of African Civilizations* 4, no. 2 (November 1982): 18. George G. M. James, *Stolen Legacy*, (Trenton: African World Press, 1992), 37-39, 42. Asa G. Hilliard, *The Maroon Within Us: Selected Essays on African American Community Socialization*, (Baltimore: Black Classic Press, 1995), 125. Maulana Karenga, *Introduction to Black Studies*, Second Edition, (Los Angeles: University of Sankore Press, 1993), 79-87, 103-109, 120, 144. Maulana Karenga, *Maat: The Moral Ideal in Ancient Egypt*, (Los Angeles: University of Sankore Press, 2006), 35, 137, 318. Benjamin Tetteh, "2019: Year of Return for African Diaspora," *African Renewal: Dec. 2018 – Mar. 2019*, https://www.un.org/africarenewal/magazine/december-2018-march-2019/2019-year-return-african-diaspora, Accessed 8 October 2020. Miriam Lichtheim, *Ancient Egyptian Literature*, Volume I, (Los Angeles: University of California Press, 1975), 51. E. A. Wallis Budge, *The Book of Kings*, Volume I, Dynasties I-XIX, (London: Kegan Paul, Trench, Trubner & Co., Ltd., 1908), 3, 14, 38, 44, 65, 106, 155. E. A. Wallis Budge, *The Book of Kings*, Volume II, Dynasties XX-XXX, (London: Kegan Paul, Trench, Trubner & Co., Ltd., 1908), 21, 70, 91, 107, 111. E. A. Wallis Budge, *A History of Egypt*, Volume I, (London: Kegan Paul, Trench, Trubner & Co., Ltd., 1902), 162-165, 179. Mine in parentheses. E. A. Wallis Budge, *Egypt*, (New York: Henry Holt and Company, 1925), 39. George the Syncellus does not include a classification under the heading *Spirits of the Dead* in his own version of the period when the Gods and Demi-Gods ruled Kemet. W. G. Waddell, *Manetho*, (Cambridge: Harvard University Press, 1964), 17-21, 229 [ ] brackets mine. Bob Brier, *The History of Ancient Egypt: Course Guidebook*, (Chantilly: The Great Courses, 1999), 146-147. Marc Van De Mieroop, *A History of Ancient Egypt*, (Malden: Wiley-Blackwell, 2011), 290. A. Abu Bakr, "Pharaonic Egypt," in *General History of Africa, II: Ancient Civilizations of Africa*, ed. G. Mokhtar, (Berkeley: University of California Press, 1981), 84. Felix Guirand, *Larousse Encyclopedia of Mythology*, (New York: Prometheus Press, 1960), 16. Edwin Murphy, *The Antiquities of Egypt: A Translation with Notes of Book I of the Library of History of Diodorus Siculus*, (New Brunswick: Transaction Publishers, 1990), 28, 56-57. George Rawlinson, *History of Herodotus*, In Four Volumes, Volume 1, (London: John Murray, 1862), 138 (note 8), 139. The Twelve Gods are: Osir, Iset, Heru, Nebt-Het, Seth, Het-Heru, Montu, Atum, Shu, Tefnyut, Geb, Nyut. D. M. Murdock, *Christ in Egypt: The Horus-Jesus Connection*, (Seattle: Stellar House Publishing, 2009), 263. *See* also E. A. Wallis Budge, *A History of Egypt*, Volume IV, (New York: Oxford University Press, 1902), 22. Tarík Karenga, *The Pharaohs' 5 Laws of Success*, First Edition, (Union City: Amenism, Inc., 2022), 31, 41, 57. Both Kemet and Amenism began in Abyssinia (*i.e.*, ancient Ethiopia). Additionally, inherent in Kemetan history, which spans more than 50,000 years, is the religion of Amenism, faithfully making Amenism the oldest religion in the world. Note: B.Z.T. means before Zep Tepi. Z.T.E. means Zep Tepi Era (*i.e.*, the time of and after Zep Tepi; hence, Zep Tepi occurs only once). Ptah (Kemetan) = Hephaistos (Greek); Ra (Kemetan) = Helios (Greek); Geb (Kemetan) = Kronos (Greek). ***Northern culmination and southern culmination dates for Sahu (which was associated with Osir) and start dates for the Age of Leo according to Amenism differ slightly from those given by author Thomas Brophy. *See* Thomas G. Brophy, *The Origin Map: Discovery of a Prehistoric, Megalithic, Astrophysical Map and Sculpture of the Universe*, (New York: Writers Club Press, 2002), 19, 97, 99.

# CONCLUSION

Aside from providing us with a better understanding of who we are in relation to God, one of the chief purposes of the calendar and Zodiac is to facilitate the harmonization of human activity not only with the Will of God, but also with the seasons of the year and thus with the movement of the stars in the sky above (*see* Table 8).[1] Additionally, the telling feature of the traditional "Sun in" (*i.e.*, Soul in) dates associated with each sign of the Zodiac is that without changing their relative position to one another and by matching them with the reverse numerical order of the signs of the Zodiac as defined by precession, their former alignment with the fall and spring equinoxes as well as with the summer and winter solstices consequently has been restored, so that the signs of the Zodiac once again correspond to our ancient system of agriculture, our religion, our calendar and to the specific astronomical events discussed above that speak to how God prophesied and recorded the indelible history of his own birth, life, death and resurrection in the very workings of the universe that he himself created. "Live in Truth!"[2]

**Table 8: Amenist Theological Perspectives on the Stages of Life**

| Perspective of: | Stage 1 | Stage 2 | Stage 3 | Stage 4 |
|---|---|---|---|---|
| **the Seasons** | Shemu | Shemu | Akhet | Pert |
| **the Stations of the Sun** | Summer Solstice | Fall Equinox | Winter Solstice | Spring Equinox |

---

1. Our body is a host for the spirit of God (*e.g.*, the spirit of God that dwells within us). We are therefore both the host and the offspring of God (*i.e.*, we are both human and divine).

2. "Live in Truth" is an ancient Kemetan aphorism. Tarík Karenga, *The Pharaohs' 5 Laws of Success*, First Edition, (Union City: Amenism, Inc., 2022), 162 note 16. Correctly matching the existing twelve groups of dates with their respective zodiacal signs in reverse numerical order as defined by precession is easily achieved. First, arrange the signs of the Zodiac in a circular configuration resembling the circular Zodiac at Dendera, making sure to position the zodiacal sign Aries at the east end of the configuration (*i.e.*, on the right), and Libra at the west end (*i.e.*, on the left), which will result in the alignment of the zodiacal sign Capricorn with the north, and Kheper with the south. Next, using a separate but transparent medium, superimpose each group of dates over the zodiacal sign with which it is currently matched. Third, rotate forward a half of a revolution (*i.e.*, flip over forward) the transparent medium containing the existing twelve groups of dates to correctly match them with their respective zodiacal signs in reverse numerical order. Now, notice that as the months of the year advance forward, the signs of the zodiac move backwards in reverse numerical order to that in which they appear in the night sky as viewed from earth, which accurately mirrors precession. Notice also that Libra and Aries are the only two zodiacal signs whose dates remain the same. *See* Table 6. Note: Scripture is written in God's creation as well as in books and on stone.

| the Periods of the Sun | Ra<br><br>[12 p.m. Noon] | Atum<br><br>[6 p.m. Evening] | Kheper-Ra<br><br>[12 a.m. Morning] | Heru-Khuti<br><br>[6 a.m. Sunrise] *i.e.,* Heru "of the two Horizons"[3] |
|---|---|---|---|---|
| **the Sun** | Birth | Death | New birth [*i.e.,* Rebirth] | Resurrection and Ascension |
| **Osir** | Birth [Emerges from Ñun in Amenta and then enters into the world] | Death | *Spiritual Revival* | Resurrection and Ascension |
| **Iset** | Birth [Emerges from Ñun in Amenta and then enters into the world] | Recovers the body of Osir | Finds, rejoins, spiritually revives, and conjoins in spirit with Osir, resulting in the virgin birth of Heru[4] | Resurrects Osir |
| **Heru** | Birth [Emerges from Ñun in Amenta; Heru (as an Elder) in the North, the eldest of the two Heru-urs, who are in fact one and the same] | -- | Conceived and born of his virgin mother Iset.<br><br>[Heru transforms himself from Heru (as a child) into Heru (as a man), and then into Heru (as an Elder) in the South, and becomes the "avenger of his father"][5] | Heru (as an Elder) awakens and raises his father to his feet. [Heru becomes Heru-Smai-Taui *i.e.,* "the uniter of the Two Lands," namely, Upper Kemet in the South and Lower Kemet in the North][6] |

3. E. A. Wallis Budge, *The Book of the Dead: The Papyrus of Ani in the British Museum*, (London: British Museum, 1895), 246 (note 6). E. A. Wallis Budge, *From Fetish to God in Ancient Egypt*, (New York: Dover Publications, Inc., 1988), 220.

4. Tarík Karenga, *The Pharaohs' 5 Laws of Success*, First Edition, (Union City: Amenism, Inc., 2022), 17.

5. E. A. Wallis Budge, *The Gods of the Egyptians: Or, Studies in Egyptian Mythology*, Volume I, (London: Methuen & Company, 1904), 467-468. E. A. Wallis Budge, *The Mummy: A Handbook of Egyptian Funerary Archaeology*, Second Edition, Revised & Greatly Enlarged, (London: Cambridge University Press, 1925), 359. E. A. Wallis Budge, *From Fetish to God in Ancient Egypt*, (New York: Dover Publications, Inc., 1988), 222. cf. Felix Guirand, *Larousse Encyclopedia of Mythology*, (New York: Prometheus Press, 1960), 22.

6. E. A. Wallis Budge, *From Fetish to God in Ancient Egypt*, (New York: Dover Publications, Inc., 1988), 220. E.

| | | | | |
|---|---|---|---|---|
| **the Ba (*i.e.*, the soul)** | Emergence from Ñun (nothing) and passage from the realm of spirit into the physical realm[7] | Entrance into a human host [*Spiritually Unborn*] | Emergence above human host [*i.e.*, Birth] | Departure from fallen human host [Resurrection and ascension of the soul of the deceased and *former* Pharaoh; renewed activity on earth of the soul of the *new* king] |
| **the Khat (*i.e.*, the body)** | Conception | Birth | Development | Death [The body of the deceased and *former* Pharaoh is embalmed and entombed; the body of the *new* king is that of a full-grown adult] |
| **the Pharaoh** | Conception | *Spiritual Crucifixion* followed by Divine Birth | *Spiritual Revival* and *Spiritual Rebirth* [The *new* king is rendered the very person of Heru, reaches spiritual maturity, and then becomes spiritually equipped; *i.e.*, the *new* king comes forth as the newborn Sun][8] | *Spiritual Resurrection* [Resurrection proper of the deceased and *former* Pharaoh, who ascends to heaven and is assimilated to Osir; however, the *new* king rules on earth as Heru and continues the *works of his father* Osir] |

---

A. Wallis Budge, *The Gods of the Egyptians: Or, Studies in Egyptian Mythology*, Volume I, (London: Methuen & Company, 1904), 472-473. Felix Guirand, *Larousse Encyclopedia of Mythology*, (New York: Prometheus Press, 1960), 22-23. *See also* E. A. Wallis Budge, *An Egyptian Hieroglyphic Dictionary: In Two Volumes*, Volume I, (London: John Murray, 1920), 505a.

    7. Ra brought himself into being; but, the Kemetans "are said to have been produced by the tears of Ra (*i.e.*, the tears of the soul) . . . *i.e.*, the sun." E. A. Wallis Budge, *The Gods of the Egyptians: Or, Studies in Egyptian Mythology*, Volume I, (London: Methuen & Company, 1904), 305, 312. Mine in parentheses.

    8. Tarík Karenga, *The Pharaohs' 5 Laws of Success*, First Edition, (Union City: Amenism, Inc., 2022), 16-17, 19, 21. *See* the terms *spiritual revival* and *spiritual rebirth*, in Tarík Karenga, *Review of the Kemetan Mystery System*, First Edition, (Union City: Amenism, Inc., in press). *See also* "Stage 3" above.

# PLATES

# PLATE 1

## Shemu: Season of Inundation (Summer)

**1. Mesut Ra**

**2. Tekhi**

**3. Paen Aopet**

**4. Het-Heru**

## Akhet: Season of Sowing (Winter)

**5. Ka Hera Ka**

**6. Ta Aobyti**

**7. Makhiar**

**8. Paen Amenhotep**

## Pert: Season of Growing and Harvesting (Spring)

**9. Paen Rennutet**

**10. Paen Khonsu**

**11. Paen Aynit**

**12. Ap Ap**

**Oup Renpet**

**Kemetan Calendar and Zodiac With Observed Holy Days: Year 52580**
(Gregorian June 25, 2019 - June 24, 2020)

45

# PLATE 2

## Shemu: Season of Inundation (Summer)

### 1. Mesut Ra

| K | 1 | 2 | 3 | 4 | 5 | 6 | 7 | 8 | 9 | 10 |
|---|---|---|---|---|---|---|---|---|---|----|
| G | 25 | 26 | 27 | 28 | 29 | 30 | jul | 2 | 3 | 4 |
| K | 11 | 12 | 13 | 14 | 15 | 16 | 17 | 18 | 19 | 20 |
| G | 5 | 6 | 7 | 8 | 9 | 10 | 11 | 12 | 13 | 14 |
| K | 21 | 22 | 23 | 24 | 25 | 26 | 27 | 28 | 29 | 30 |
| G | 15 | 16 | 17 | 18 | 19 | 20 | 21 | 22 | 23 | 24 |

*Sagittarius*

### 2. Tekhi

| K | 1 | 2 | 3 | 4 | 5 | 6 | 7 | 8 | 9 | 10 |
|---|---|---|---|---|---|---|---|---|---|----|
| G | 25 | 26 | 27 | 28 | 29 | 30 | 31 | aug | 2 | 3 |
| K | 11 | 12 | 13 | 14 | 15 | 16 | 17 | 18 | 19 | 20 |
| G | 4 | 5 | 6 | 7 | 8 | 9 | 10 | 11 | 12 | 13 |
| K | 21 | 22 | 23 | 24 | 25 | 26 | 27 | 28 | 29 | 30 |
| G | 14 | 15 | 16 | 17 | 18 | 19 | 20 | 21 | 22 | 23 |

*Scorpio*

### 3. Paen Aopet

| K | 1 | 2 | 3 | 4 | 5 | 6 | 7 | 8 | 9 | 10 |
|---|---|---|---|---|---|---|---|---|---|----|
| G | 24 | 25 | 26 | 27 | 28 | 29 | 30 | 31 | sep | 2 |
| K | 11 | 12 | 13 | 14 | 15 | 16 | 17 | 18 | 19 | 20 |
| G | 3 | 4 | 5 | 6 | 7 | 8 | 9 | 10 | 11 | 12 |
| K | 21 | 22 | 23 | 24 | 25 | 26 | 27 | 28 | 29 | 30 |
| G | 13 | 14 | 15 | 16 | 17 | 18 | 19 | 20 | 21 | 22 |

*Libra*

### 4. Het-Heru

| K | 1 | 2 | 3 | 4 | 5 | 6 | 7 | 8 | 9 | 10 |
|---|---|---|---|---|---|---|---|---|---|----|
| G | 23 | 24 | 25 | 26 | 27 | 28 | 29 | 30 | oct | 2 |
| K | 11 | 12 | 13 | 14 | 15 | 16 | 17 | 18 | 19 | 20 |
| G | 3 | 4 | 5 | 6 | 7 | 8 | 9 | 10 | 11 | 12 |
| K | 21 | 22 | 23 | 24 | 25 | 26 | 27 | 28 | 29 | 30 |
| G | 13 | 14 | 15 | 16 | 17 | 18 | 19 | 20 | 21 | 22 |

*Taurus*

## Akhet: Season of Sowing (Winter)

### 5. Ka Hera Ka

| K | 1 | 2 | 3 | 4 | 5 | 6 | 7 | 8 | 9 | 10 |
|---|---|---|---|---|---|---|---|---|---|----|
| G | 23 | 24 | 25 | 26 | 27 | 28 | 29 | 30 | 31 | nv |
| K | 11 | 12 | 13 | 14 | 15 | 16 | 17 | 18 | 19 | 20 |
| G | 2 | 3 | 4 | 5 | 6 | 7 | 8 | 9 | 10 | 11 |
| K | 21 | 22 | 23 | 24 | 25 | 26 | 27 | 28 | 29 | 30 |
| G | 12 | 13 | 14 | 15 | 16 | 17 | 18 | 19 | 20 | 21 |

*Virgo*

### 6. Ta Aobyti

| K | 1 | 2 | 3 | 4 | 5 | 6 | 7 | 8 | 9 | 10 |
|---|---|---|---|---|---|---|---|---|---|----|
| G | 22 | 23 | 24 | 25 | 26 | 27 | 28 | 29 | 30 | dc |
| K | 11 | 12 | 13 | 14 | 15 | 16 | 17 | 18 | 19 | 20 |
| G | 2 | 3 | 4 | 5 | 6 | 7 | 8 | 9 | 10 | 11 |
| K | 21 | 22 | 23 | 24 | 25 | 26 | 27 | 28 | 29 | 30 |
| G | 12 | 13 | 14 | 15 | 16 | 17 | 18 | 19 | 20 | 21 |

*Leo*

### 7. Makhiar

| K | 1 | 2 | 3 | 4 | 5 | 6 | 7 | 8 | 9 | 10 |
|---|---|---|---|---|---|---|---|---|---|----|
| G | 22 | 23 | 24 | 25 | 26 | 27 | 28 | 29 | 30 | 31 |
| K | 11 | 12 | 13 | 14 | 15 | 16 | 17 | 18 | 19 | 20 |
| G | jan | 2 | 3 | 4 | 5 | 6 | 7 | 8 | 9 | 10 |
| K | 21 | 22 | 23 | 24 | 25 | 26 | 27 | 28 | 29 | 30 |
| G | 11 | 12 | 13 | 14 | 15 | 16 | 17 | 18 | 19 | 20 |

*Kheper*

### 8. Paen Amenhotep

| K | 1 | 2 | 3 | 4 | 5 | 6 | 7 | 8 | 9 | 10 |
|---|---|---|---|---|---|---|---|---|---|----|
| G | 21 | 22 | 23 | 24 | 25 | 26 | 27 | 28 | 29 | 30 |
| K | 11 | 12 | 13 | 14 | 15 | 16 | 17 | 18 | 19 | 20 |
| G | 31 | feb | 2 | 3 | 4 | 5 | 6 | 7 | 8 | 9 |
| K | 21 | 22 | 23 | 24 | 25 | 26 | 27 | 28 | 29 | 30 |
| G | 10 | 11 | 12 | 13 | 14 | 15 | 16 | 17 | 18 | 19 |

*Gemini*

## Pert: Season of Growing and Harvesting (Spring)

### 9. Paen Renñutet

| K | 1 | 2 | 3 | 4 | 5 | 6 | 7 | 8 | 9 | 10 |
|---|---|---|---|---|---|---|---|---|---|----|
| G | 20 | 21 | 22 | 23 | 24 | 25 | 26 | 27 | 28 | mr |
| K | 11 | 12 | 13 | 14 | 15 | 16 | 17 | 18 | 19 | 20 |
| G | 2 | 3 | 4 | 5 | 6 | 7 | 8 | 9 | 10 | 11 |
| K | 21 | 22 | 23 | 24 | 25 | 26 | 27 | 28 | 29 | 30 |
| G | 12 | 13 | 14 | 15 | 16 | 17 | 18 | 19 | 20 | 21 |

*Aries*

### 10. Paen Khonsu

| K | 1 | 2 | 3 | 4 | 5 | 6 | 7 | 8 | 9 | 10 |
|---|---|---|---|---|---|---|---|---|---|----|
| G | 22 | 23 | 24 | 25 | 26 | 27 | 28 | 29 | 30 | 31 |
| K | 11 | 12 | 13 | 14 | 15 | 16 | 17 | 18 | 19 | 20 |
| G | apr | 2 | 3 | 4 | 5 | 6 | 7 | 8 | 9 | 10 |
| K | 21 | 22 | 23 | 24 | 25 | 26 | 27 | 28 | 29 | 30 |
| G | 11 | 12 | 13 | 14 | 15 | 16 | 17 | 18 | 19 | 20 |

*Pisces*

### 11. Paen Aynit

| K | 1 | 2 | 3 | 4 | 5 | 6 | 7 | 8 | 9 | 10 |
|---|---|---|---|---|---|---|---|---|---|----|
| G | 21 | 22 | 23 | 24 | 25 | 26 | 27 | 28 | 29 | 30 |
| K | 11 | 12 | 13 | 14 | 15 | 16 | 17 | 18 | 19 | 20 |
| G | my | 2 | 3 | 4 | 5 | 6 | 7 | 8 | 9 | 10 |
| K | 21 | 22 | 23 | 24 | 25 | 26 | 27 | 28 | 29 | 30 |
| G | 11 | 12 | 13 | 14 | 15 | 16 | 17 | 18 | 19 | 20 |

*Aquarius*

### 12. Ap Ap

| K | 1 | 2 | 3 | 4 | 5 | 6 | 7 | 8 | 9 | 10 |
|---|---|---|---|---|---|---|---|---|---|----|
| G | 21 | 22 | 23 | 24 | 25 | 26 | 27 | 28 | 29 | 30 |
| K | 11 | 12 | 13 | 14 | 15 | 16 | 17 | 18 | 19 | 20 |
| G | 31 | jun | 2 | 3 | 4 | 5 | 6 | 7 | 8 | 9 |
| K | 21 | 22 | 23 | 24 | 25 | 26 | 27 | 28 | 29 | 30 |
| G | 10 | 11 | 12 | 13 | 14 | 15 | 16 | 17 | 18 | 19 |

### Oup Renpet

| K | 1 | 2 | 3 | 4 | 5 |
|---|---|---|---|---|---|
| G | 20 | 21 | 22 | 23 | 24 |

*Capricorn*

## Kemetan Calendar and Zodiac With Observed Holy Days: Year 52581
### (Gregorian June 25, 2020 - June 24, 2021)

46

## PLATE 3

### The Kemetan Circular Zodiac in the Reemergent Kingdom[1]

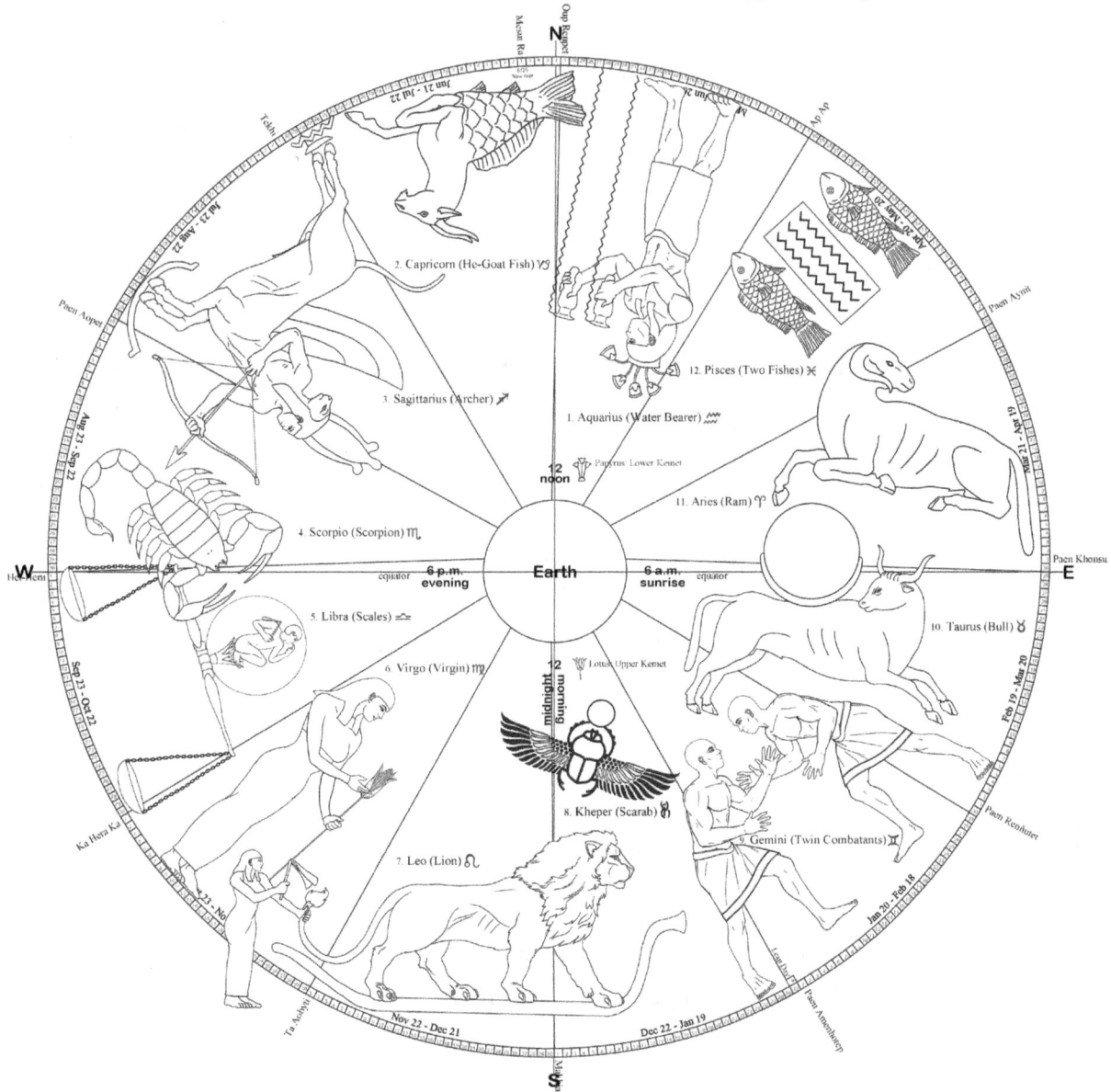

1. After the circular Zodiac at Dendera in ancient Kemet; *see* E. A. Wallis Budge, *The Gods of the Egyptians: Or, Studies in Egyptian Mythology*, Volume II, (London: Methuen & Company, 1904), 314-315. Napoleon Bonaparte, *Description De L'Egypte*, Tome 4, Planches, (Paris: De L'Imprimerie Royale, 1817), Plates 20-21. Vivant Denon, *Voyage Dans La Basse Et La Haute Egypte*, Planches, (London: M. Peltier, 1802), Plates XLVIII-XLIX. Sir W. Drummond, *The Oedipus Judaicus*, (London: A. J. Valpy, Took's Coury, Chancery Lane, 1811), Plates 6-7. CDC, *Pictorial Keys to Arthropods, Reptiles, Birds and Mammals of Public Health Significance*, (Atlanta: U.S. Department of Health, Education, and Welfare, 1966), 23. William Henry Goodyear, *The Grammar of the Lotus*, (London: Sampson Low, Marston & Company, 1891), 3. Starder, *Hand Drawn Corn Vector Design 01* [Digital File], retrieved on 11/03/2020 from https://freedesignfile.com/153944-hand-drawn-corn-vector-design-01/. Written symbols of the Zodiac in Frances Sakoian and Louis S. Acker, *The Astrologer's Handbook*, (New York: Collins Reference, 1973), 14. Hieratic symbol for Kheper in Arnold Buffum Chace, *The Rhind Mathematical Papyrus*, (Oberlin: Mathematical Association of America, 1979), 125. *See* also E. A. Wallis Budge, *An Egyptian Hieroglyphic Dictionary: In Two Volumes*, Volume I, (London: John Murray, 1920), cxxii, cxxiii, 542a. G. Woolliscroft Rhead, The *Principles of Design*, (London: B. T. Batsford, 1905), 162. Other Graphic artists: Allen Totingski and Tarík Karenga. Profiles: Soma Karenga, Leyda Patterson, Saidi Karenga, Enrique Karenga, and Tarík Karenga.

## PLATE 4

**Heru's Three Stages of Development That Correspond to the**

**Three Stages of** *Spiritual Rebirth*[2]

| **Heru (as a child)** | **Heru (as a man)** | **Heru (as an Elder)** |
|---|---|---|

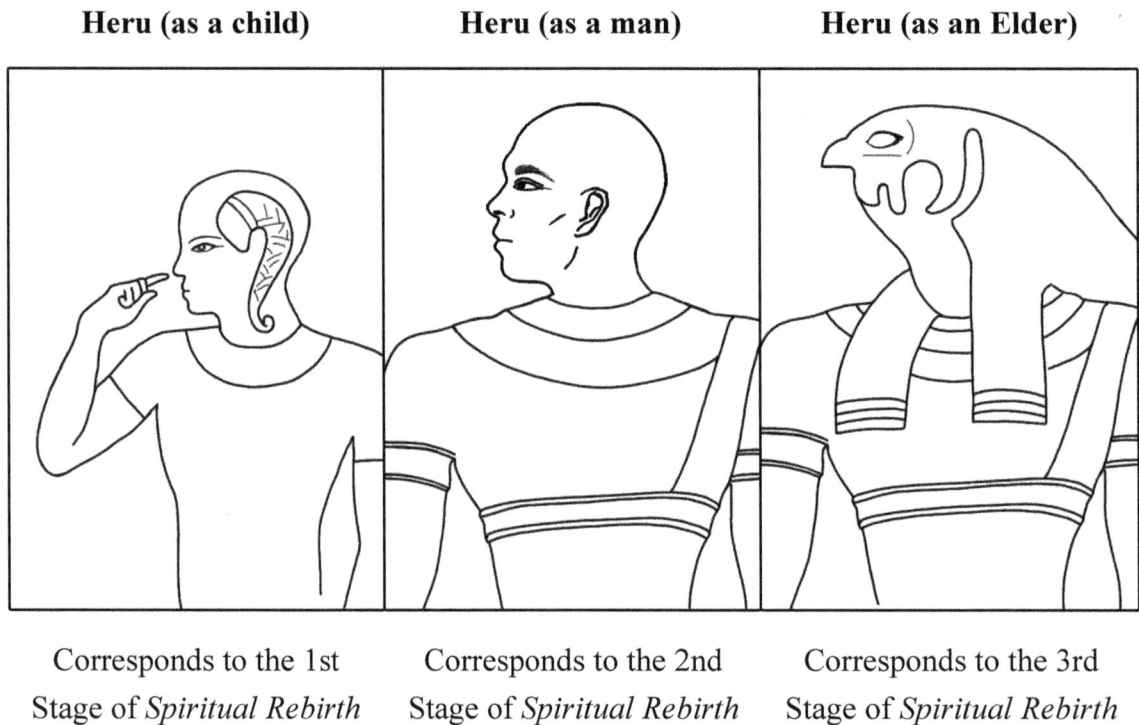

| Corresponds to the 1st Stage of *Spiritual Rebirth* | Corresponds to the 2nd Stage of *Spiritual Rebirth* | Corresponds to the 3rd Stage of *Spiritual Rebirth* |
|---|---|---|

2.  Napoleon Bonaparte, *Description De L'Egypte*, Tome 4, Planches, (Paris: De L'Imprimerie Royale, 1817), Plate 28(4). E. A. Wallis Budge, *The Gods of the Egyptians: Or, Studies in Egyptian Mythology*, Volume I, (London: Methuen & Company, 1904), 468-469, Plate 28. Ippolito Rosellini, *I Monumenti Dell' Egitto e Della Nubia*, Tomo Terzo, Monumenti Del Culto, (Pisa: Presso Niccolo Capurro, 1844), Plate LIII (4).

# PLATE 5
## AMENIST FOUNDATIONAL HOLY DAYS
[Official Religious Observance Dates]

| | | | |
|---|---|---|---|
| New Year | Mesut Ra 1st | | June 25th (Gregorian) |
| *Osir Enters the World; Birth of Ra* | | | |
| First Appearance of Sepdta | Tekhi 16th | *Nile Flood Stage Begins* | August 9th (Gregorian) |
| *i.e., Heliacal Rising of Sepdta* | | | |
| Opening of the Canals Ceremony | Tekhi 17th | | August 10th (Gregorian) |
| Death of Osir | Paen Aopet 30th | *Fall Equinox* | September 22nd (Gregorian) |
| *Spiritual Crucifixion* (Pharaoh) | | | |
| Divine Birth of the Pharaoh | Het-Heru 1st | | September 23rd (Gregorian) |
| (Symbolic) Death of Osir | Het-Heru 17th | *Nile Begins to Fall* | October 9th (Gregorian) |
| *as the Personification of the Falling Nile* | | | |
| Passion Play and Festival of Osir | Ka Hera Ka 17th | | November 8th (Gregorian) |
| *14-Day Festival and Pilgrimage* | | | |
| Three-Day Search of Iset | Ta Aobyti 26th | | December 17th (Gregorian) |
| *Spiritual Revival* of Osir | Ta Aobyti 29th | *Nile Flood Stage Ends* | December 20th (Gregorian) |
| *Spiritual Revival* (Pharaoh) | | | |
| Conception of Heru | Ta Aobyti 30th | *Winter Solstice* | December 21st (Gregorian) |
| Birth of Heru (as a newborn babe) | Makhiar 4th | *Day of the Great* | December 25th (Gregorian) |
| *Spiritual Rebirth* (Pharaoh) | | *Coming Forth* | |
| Three-Day Battle of Heru and Seth | Paen Amenhotep 26th | | *February 15th (Gregorian) |
| Entombment of Osir | Paen Renñutet 26th | | March 17th (Gregorian) |
| *Entombment of former Pharaoh* | | | |
| Resurrection of Osir | Paen Renñutet 30th | *Spring Equinox* | March 21st (Gregorian) |
| *Resurrection (proper) of former Pharaoh* | | | |
| Accession of the *new* king | Paen Khonsu 1st | | March 22nd (Gregorian) |
| *Spiritual Resurrection* of the *new* king | Paen Khonsu 4th | | March 25th (Gregorian) |
| Disappearance of Sepdta | Ap Ap 11th | | May 31st (Gregorian) |
| *70-Day Embalming of former Pharaoh* | | | |
| Birthday of Osir | Oup Renpet 1st | *Nile Begins to Rise* | June 20th (Gregorian) |
| Birthday of Heru (as an Elder) | Oup Renpet 2nd | *Summer Solstice* | June 21st (Gregorian) |
| Birthday of Seth | Oup Renpet 3rd | | June 22nd (Gregorian) |
| *Jurisdiction of the Great Divine Ennead* | | | |
| Birthday of Iset | Oup Renpet 4th | | June 23rd (Gregorian) |
| Birthday of Nebt-Het | Oup Renpet 5th | | June 24th (Gregorian) |

*Gregorian calendar date for non leap year (Kemetan); but, for leap year (Kemetan), use February 16th (Gregorian)

# PLATE 6

## THE KEMETAN CALENDAR

An ordinary year consists of 365 days, but a leap year has 366 days.
"A leap year is a year whose number is exactly divisible by 4," but not by 128 unless its number is also exactly divisible by 80,000.[1]

## DETERMINING THE DAY OF THE WEEK

**Step 1:** take the year preceding the (target year > or = 2). If the year is divisible by 2 then (without figuring in leap days) the day of the week of the first day of the target year initially will be Ra. If the year is not divisible by 2 then (without figuring in leap days) the day of the week of the first day of the target year initially will be Mut.

**Step 2:** take the year preceding the target year and find the number of leap days by using the Kemetan calendar leap year method.

**Step 3:** divide the number of leap days by 10. If the resultant figure does not include a decimal point, then count 10 leap days forward beginning on Ra or Mut as determined above. If the resultant figure includes a decimal point, then count the number of leap days forward based on the number to the right of the decimal point beginning on Ra or Mut as determined above.

**Step 4:** the very next day is the day of the week of the first day of the target year.

---

1. *See* "leap year" in Webster's New World Dictionary & Thesaurus, Version 2.0, Build #25, Accent Software International, Macmillan Publishers, 1998.

## PLATE 7

Mesut Ra 52580

| Ra | Khnum | Bast | Sobek | Tauret | Mut | Amen | Sekhmet | Ptah | Hapi |
|---|---|---|---|---|---|---|---|---|---|
|  |  |  |  |  |  |  |  |  | 1 New Year; Birth of Ra; Osir enters the world; first day of Shemu — Tu•06•25•19 |
| 2 | 3 | 4 | 5 | 6 | 7 | 8 | 9 | 10 | 11 |
| We•06•26•19 | Th•06•27•19 | Fr•06•28•19 | Sa•06•29•19 | Su•06•30•19 | Mo•07•01•19 | Tu•07•02•19 | We•07•03•19 | Th•07•04•19 | Fr•07•05•19 |
| 12 | 13 | 14 | 15 | 16 | 17 | 18 | 19 | 20 | 21 |
| Sa•07•06•19 | Su•07•07•19 | Mo•07•08•19 | Tu•07•09•19 | We•07•10•19 | Th•07•11•19 | Fr•07•12•19 | Sa•07•13•19 | Su•07•14•19 | Mo•07•15•19 |
| 22 | 23 | 24 | 25 | 26 | 27 | 28 Sagittarius begins | 29 | 30 |  |
| Tu•07•16•19 | We•07•17•19 | Th•07•18•19 | Fr•07•19•19 | Sa•07•20•19 | Su•07•21•19 | Mo•07•22•19 | Tu•07•23•19 | We•07•24•19 |  |

## PLATE 8

52580

Tekhi

| Ra | Khnum | Bast | Sobek | Tauret | Mut | Amen | Sekhmet | Ptah | Hapi |
|---|---|---|---|---|---|---|---|---|---|
| | | | | | | | | | 1<br>Th•07•25•19 |
| 2<br>Fr•07•26•19 | 3<br>Sa•07•27•19 | 4<br>Su•07•28•19 | 5<br>Mo•07•29•19 | 6<br>Tu•07•30•19 | 7<br>We•07•31•19 | 8<br>Th•08•01•19 | 9<br>Fr•08•02•19 | 10<br>Sa•08•03•19 | 11<br>Su•08•04•19 |
| 12<br>Mo•08•05•19 | 13<br>Tu•08•06•19 | 14<br>We•08•07•19 | 15<br>Th•08•08•19 | 16 First Appearance of Sepdta; (Official Observance); Nile Flood Stage Begins<br>Tu•07•30•19 | 17 Opening of the Canals<br>We•07•31•19 | 18<br>Th•08•01•19 | 19<br>Fr•08•02•19 | 20<br>Tu•08•13•19 | 21<br>We•08•14•19 |
| 22<br>Th•08•15•19 | 23<br>Fr•08•16•19 | 24<br>Sa•08•17•19 | 25<br>Su•08•18•19 | 26<br>Mo•08•19•19 | 27<br>Tu•08•20•19 | 28<br>We•08•21•19 | 29<br>Th•08•22•19 | 30 Scorpio begins<br>Fr•08•23•19 | |

# PLATE 9

| Ra | Khnum | Bast | Sobek | Tauret | Mut | Amen | Sekhmet | Ptah | Hapi |
|---|---|---|---|---|---|---|---|---|---|
| | | | | | | | | | 1 |
| | | | | | | | | | Sa•08•24•19 |
| 2 | 3 | 4 | 5 | 6 | 7 | 8 | 9 | 10 | 11 |
| Su•08•25•19 | Mo•08•26•19 | Tu•08•27•19 | We•08•28•19 | Th•08•29•19 | Fr•08•30•19 | Sa•08•31•19 | Su•09•01•19 | Mo•09•02•19 | Tu•09•03•19 |
| 12 | 13 | 14 | 15 | 16 | 17 | 18 | 19 | 20 | 21 |
| We•09•04•19 | Th•09•05•19 | Fr•09•06•19 | Sa•09•07•19 | Su•09•08•19 | Mo•09•09•19 | Tu•09•10•19 | We•09•11•19 | Th•09•12•19 | Fr•09•13•19 |
| 22 | 23 | 24 | 25 | 26 | 27 | 28 | 29 | 30 Death *of Osir, Sp. Crucifixion of (Pharaoh)* | |
| Sa•09•14•19 | Su•09•15•19 | Mo•09•16•19 | Tu•09•17•19 | We•09•18•19 | Th•09•19•19 | Fr•09•20•19 | Sa•09•21•19 | Su•09•22•19 | |

## PLATE 10

52580

**Month: Het-Heru**

| Hapi | Ra | Khnum | Bast | Sobek | Tauret | Mut | Amen | Sekhmet | Ptah |
|---|---|---|---|---|---|---|---|---|---|
| 1 — Mo•09•23•19 — Divine Birth (Pharaoh); Libra begins | 2 — Tu•09•24•19 | 3 — We•09•25•19 | 4 — Th•09•26•19 | 5 — Fr•09•27•19 | 6 — Sa•09•28•19 | 7 — Su•09•29•19 | 8 — Mo•09•30•19 | 9 — Tu•10•01•19 | 10 — We•10•02•19 |
| 11 — Th•10•03•19 | 12 — Fr•10•04•19 | 13 — Sa•10•05•19 | 14 — Su•10•06•19 | 15 — Mo•10•07•19 | 16 — Tu•10•08•19 | 17 — We•10•09•19 — Nile Begins to Fall | 18 — Th•10•10•19 | 19 — Fr•10•11•19 | 20 — Sa•10•12•19 |
| 21 — Su•10•13•19 | 22 — Mo•10•14•19 | 23 — Tu•10•15•19 | 24 — We•10•16•19 | 25 — Th•10•17•19 | 26 — Fr•10•18•19 | 27 — Sa•10•19•19 | 28 — Su•10•20•19 | 29 — Mo•10•21•19 | 30 — Tu•10•22•19 |

# PLATE 11

| Ra | Khnum | Bast | Sobek | Tauret | Mut | Amen | Sekhmet | Ptah | Hapi |
|---|---|---|---|---|---|---|---|---|---|
|  |  |  |  |  |  |  |  |  | 1 First day of Akhet; Virgo begins<br>We•10•23•19 |
| 2<br>Th•10•24•19 | 3<br>Fr•10•25•19 | 4<br>Sa•10•26•19 | 5<br>Su•10•27•19 | 6<br>Mo•10•28•19 | 7<br>Tu•10•29•19 | 8<br>We•10•30•19 | 9<br>Th•10•31•19 | 10<br>Fr•11•01•19 | 11<br>Sa•11•02•19 |
| 12<br>Su•11•03•19 | 13<br>Mo•11•04•19 | 14<br>Tu•11•05•19 | 15<br>We•11•06•19 | 16<br>Th•11•07•19 | 17 (1) Passion Play and Festival of Osir; 14-day Pilgrimage<br>Fr•11•08•19 | 18 (2)<br>Sa•11•09•19 | 19 (3)<br>Su•11•10•19 | 20 (4)<br>Mo•11•11•19 | 21 (5)<br>Tu•11•12•19 |
| 22 (6)<br>We•11•13•19 | 23 (7)<br>Th•11•14•19 | 24 (8)<br>Fr•11•15•19 | 25 (9)<br>Sa•11•16•19 | 26 (10)<br>Su•11•17•19 | 27 (11)<br>Mo•11•18•19 | 28 (12)<br>Tu•11•19•19 | 29 (13)<br>We•11•20•19 | 30 (14)<br>Th•11•21•19 |  |

## PLATE 12

52580

Ta Aobyti

| Ra | Khnum | Bast | Sobek | Tauret | Mut | Amen | Sekhmet | Ptah | Hapi |
|---|---|---|---|---|---|---|---|---|---|
| | | | | | | | | | 1 Leo begins — Fr•11•22•19 |
| Sa•11•23•19 — 2 | Su•11•24•19 — 3 | Mo•11•25•19 — 4 | Tu•11•26•19 — 5 | We•11•27•19 — 6 | Th•11•28•19 — 7 | Fr•11•29•19 — 8 | Sa•11•30•19 — 9 | Su•12•01•19 — 10 | Mo•12•02•19 — 11 |
| Tu•12•03•19 — 12 | We•12•04•19 — 13 | Th•12•05•19 — 14 | Fr•12•06•19 — 15 | Sa•12•07•19 — 16 | Su•12•08•19 — 17 | Mo•12•09•19 — 18 | Tu•12•10•19 — 19 | We•12•11•19 — 20 | Th•12•12•19 — 21 |
| Fr•12•13•19 — 22 | Sa•12•14•19 — 23 | Su•12•15•19 — 24 | Mo•12•16•19 — 25 | Tu•12•17•19 — 26 Three-Day Search of Iset | We•12•18•19 — 27 | Th•12•19•19 — 28 | Fr•12•20•19 — 29 *Spiritual Revival* of Osir; *Sp. Revival* (Pharaoh); Nile Flood Stage Ends | Sa•12•21•19 — 30 Conception of Heru | |

# PLATE 13

**Makhiar** — 52580

| | Ra | Khnum | Bast | Sobek | Tauret | Mut | Amen | Sekhmet | Ptah | Hapi |
|---|---|---|---|---|---|---|---|---|---|---|
| | | | | | | | | | | 1 Kheper begins<br>Su•12•22•19 |
| | 2<br>Mo•12•23•19 | 3<br>Tu•12•24•19 | 4 Birth of Heru (as a newborn babe); *Sp. Rebirth of (Pharaoh)*<br>We•12•25•19 | 5<br>Th•12•26•19 | 6<br>Fr•12•27•19 | 7<br>Sa•12•28•19 | 8<br>Su•12•29•19 | 9<br>Mo•12•30•19 | 10<br>Tu•12•31•19 | 11<br>We•01•01•20 |
| | 12<br>Th•01•02•20 | 13<br>Fr•01•03•20 | 14<br>Sa•01•04•20 | 15<br>Su•01•05•20 | 16<br>Mo•01•06•20 | 17<br>Tu•01•07•20 | 18<br>We•01•08•20 | 19<br>Th•01•09•20 | 20<br>Fr•01•10•20 | 21<br>Sa•01•11•20 |
| | 22<br>Su•01•12•20 | 23<br>Mo•01•13•20 | 24<br>Tu•01•14•20 | 25<br>We•01•15•20 | 26<br>Th•01•16•20 | 27<br>Fr•01•17•20 | 28<br>Sa•01•18•20 | 29<br>Su•01•19•20 | 30 Gemini begins<br>Mo•01•20•20 | 31 Leap Day<br>Tu•01•21•20 |

## PLATE 14

52580

Paen Amenhotep

| Ra | Khnum | Bast | Sobek | Tauret | Mut | Amen | Sekhmet | Ptah | Hapi |
|---|---|---|---|---|---|---|---|---|---|
| 1 | 2 | 3 | 4 | 5 | 6 | 7 | 8 | 9 | 10 |
| We•01•22•20 | Th•01•23•20 | Fr•01•24•20 | Sa•01•25•20 | Su•01•26•20 | Mo•01•27•20 | Tu•01•28•20 | We•01•29•20 | Th•01•30•20 | Fr•01•31•20 |
| 11 | 12 | 13 | 14 | 15 | 16 | 17 | 18 | 19 | 20 |
| Sa•02•01•20 | Su•02•02•20 | Mo•02•03•20 | Tu•02•04•20 | We•02•05•20 | Th•02•06•20 | Fr•02•07•20 | Sa•02•08•20 | Su•02•09•20 | Mo•02•10•20 |
| 21 | 22 | 23 | 24 | 25 | 26 Three-Day Battle: Heru and Seth | 27 | 28 | 29 | 30 Taurus begins |
| Tu•02•11•20 | We•02•12•20 | Th•02•13•20 | Fr•02•14•20 | Sa•02•15•20 | Su•02•16•20 | Mo•02•17•20 | Tu•02•18•20 | We•02•19•20 | Th•02•20•20 |

## PLATE 15

**Paen Renñutet** — 52580

| | Day | Day | Date | Day | Date | Date |
|---|---|---|---|---|---|---|
| Ra | 1 First day of Pert | 11 | Fr•02•21•20 | 21 | | Th•03•12•20 |
| Khnum | 2 | 12 | Sa•02•22•20 | 22 | | Fr•03•13•20 |
| Bast | 3 | 13 | Su•02•23•20 | 23 | | Sa•03•14•20 |
| Sobek | 4 | 14 | Mo•02•24•20 | 24 | | Su•03•15•20 |
| Tauret | 5 | 15 | Tu•02•25•20 | 25 | | Mo•03•16•20 |
| Mut | 6 | 16 | We•02•26•20 | 26 Entombment of Osir; Entombment of (former Pharaoh) | Sa•03•07•20 | Tu•03•17•20 |
| Amen | 7 | 17 | Th•02•27•20 | 27 | Su•03•08•20 | We•03•18•20 |
| Sekhmet | 8 | 18 | Fr•02•28•20 | 28 | Mo•03•09•20 | Th•03•19•20 |
| Ptah | 9 | 19 | Sa•02•29•20 | 29 | Tu•03•10•20 | Fr•03•20•20 |
| Hapi | 10 | 20 | Su•03•01•20 | 30 Resurrection of Osir; Resurrection (proper) of former Pharaoh; Aries begins | We•03•11•20 | Sa•03•21•20 |

# PLATE 16

Paen Khonsu

52580

| Ra | Khnum | Bast | Sobek | Tauret | Mut | Amen | Sekhmet | Ptah | Hapi |
|---|---|---|---|---|---|---|---|---|---|
| 1 Accession of the new king | 2 | 3 | 4 *Spiritual Resurrection of the new king* | 5 | 6 | 7 | 8 | 9 | 10 |
| Su•03•22•20 | Mo•03•23•20 | Tu•03•24•20 | We•03•25•20 | Th•03•26•20 | Fr•03•27•20 | Sa•03•28•20 | Su•03•29•20 | Mo•03•30•20 | Tu•03•31•20 |
| 11 | 12 | 13 | 14 | 15 | 16 | 17 | 18 | 19 | 20 |
| We•04•01•20 | Th•04•02•20 | Fr•04•03•20 | Sa•04•04•20 | Su•04•05•20 | Mo•04•06•20 | Tu•04•07•20 | We•04•08•20 | Th•04•09•20 | Fr•04•10•20 |
| 21 | 22 | 23 | 24 | 25 | 26 | 27 | 28 | 29 | 30 Pisces begins |
| Sa•04•11•20 | Su•04•12•20 | Mo•04•13•20 | Tu•04•14•20 | We•04•15•20 | Th•04•16•20 | Fr•04•17•20 | Sa•04•18•20 | Su•04•19•20 | Mo•04•20•20 |

# PLATE 17

| | | | | | | |
|---|---|---|---|---|---|---|
| Ra | 1 | 11 | Tu•04•21•20 | 21 | Fr•05•01•20 | Mo•05•11•20 |
| Khnum | 2 | 12 | We•04•22•20 | 22 | Sa•05•02•20 | Tu•05•12•20 |
| Bast | 3 | 13 | Th•04•23•20 | 23 | Su•05•03•20 | We•05•13•20 |
| Sobek | 4 | 14 | Fr•04•24•20 | 24 | Mo•05•04•20 | Th•05•14•20 |
| Tauret | 5 | 15 | Sa•04•25•20 | 25 | Tu•05•05•20 | Fr•05•15•20 |
| Mut | 6 | 16 | Su•04•26•20 | 26 | We•05•06•20 | Sa•05•16•20 |
| Amen | 7 | 17 | Mo•04•27•20 | 27 | Th•05•07•20 | Su•05•17•20 |
| Sekhmet | 8 | 18 | Tu•04•28•20 | 28 | Fr•05•08•20 | Mo•05•18•20 |
| Ptah | 9 | 19 | We•04•29•20 | 29 | Sa•05•09•20 | Tu•05•19•20 |
| Hapi | 10 | 20 | Th•04•30•20 | 30 | Su•05•10•20 | We•05•20•20 |

## PLATE 18

Ap Ap

52580

| Ra | Khnum | Bast | Sobek | Tauret | Mut | Amen | Sekhmet | Ptah | Hapi |
|---|---|---|---|---|---|---|---|---|---|
| 1 | 2 | 3 | 4 | 5 | 6 | 7 | 8 | 9 | 10 |
| Aquarius begins | | | | | | | | | |
| Th•05•21•20 | Fr•05•22•20 | Sa•05•23•20 | Su•05•24•20 | Mo•05•25•20 | Tu•05•26•20 | We•05•27•20 | Th•05•28•20 | Fr•05•29•20 | Sa•05•30•20 |
| 11 Disappearance of Sepdta; 70-Day Embalming of former Pharaoh | 12 | 13 | 14 | 15 | 16 | 17 | 18 | 19 | 20 |
| Su•05•31•20 | Mo•06•01•20 | Tu•06•02•20 | We•06•03•20 | Th•06•04•20 | Fr•06•05•20 | Sa•06•06•20 | Su•06•07•20 | Mo•06•08•20 | Tu•06•09•20 |
| 21 | 22 | 23 | 24 | 25 | 26 | 27 | 28 | 29 | 30 |
| We•06•10•20 | Th•06•11•20 | Fr•06•12•20 | Sa•06•13•20 | Su•06•14•20 | Mo•06•15•20 | Tu•06•16•20 | We•06•17•20 | Th•06•18•20 | Fr•06•19•20 |

## PLATE 19

**Oup Renpet (The Calendrical Five-Day Period)**

| Ra | Khnum | Bast | Sobek | Tauret | Mut | Amen | Sekhmet | Ptah | Hapi |
|---|---|---|---|---|---|---|---|---|---|
| 1 Birthday of Osir; Nile Begins to Rise <br> Sa•06•20•20 | 2 Birthday of Heru-ur (*i.e.,* Heru as an Elder) <br> Capricorn begins <br> Su•06•21•20 | 3 Birthday of Seth; "Jurisdiction of the Great Divine Enne-ad"[1] <br> Mo•06•22•20 | 4 Birthday of Iset <br> Tu•06•23•20 | 5 Birthday of Nebt-Het <br> We•06•24•20 | | | | | |
| | | | | | | | | | |
| | | | | | | | | | |
| | | | | | | | | | |
| | | | | | | | | | |

1. Maulana Karenga, Maat: The Moral Ideal in Ancient Egypt, (Los Angeles: University of Sankore Press, 2006), 206.

52580

## PLATE 20

Mesut Ra     52581

| Ra | Khnum | Bast | Sobek | Tauret | Mut | Amen | Sekhmet | Ptah | Hapi |
|---|---|---|---|---|---|---|---|---|---|
| | | | | | 1 New Year; Birth of Ra; Osir enters the world; first day of Shemu<br>Th•06•25•20 | 2<br>Fr•06•26•20 | 3<br>Sa•06•27•20 | 4<br>Su•06•28•20 | 5<br>Mo•06•29•20 |
| 6<br>Tu•06•30•20 | 7<br>We•07•01•20 | 8<br>Th•07•02•20 | 9<br>Fr•07•03•20 | 10<br>Sa•07•04•20 | 11<br>Su•07•05•20 | 12<br>Mo•07•06•20 | 13<br>Tu•07•07•20 | 14<br>We•07•08•20 | 15<br>Th•07•09•20 |
| 16<br>Fr•07•10•20 | 17<br>Sa•07•11•20 | 18<br>Su•07•12•20 | 19<br>Mo•07•13•20 | 20<br>Tu•07•14•20 | 21<br>We•07•15•20 | 22<br>Th•07•16•20 | 23<br>Fr•07•17•20 | 24<br>Sa•07•18•20 | 25<br>Su•07•19•20 |
| 26<br>Mo•07•20•20 | 27<br>Tu•07•21•20 | 28<br>We•07•22•20 | 29<br>Sagittarius begins<br>Th•07•23•20 | 30<br>Fr•07•24•20 | | | | | |

# PLATE 21

52581

|  | | | | |
|---|---|---|---|---|
| Ra | | 6 — Th•07•30•20 | 16 First Appearance of Sepdta; (Official Observance); Nile Flood Stage Begins — Su•08•09•20 | 26 — We•08•19•20 |
| Khnum | | 7 — Fr•07•31•20 | 17 Opening of the Canals — Mo•08•10•20 | 27 — Th•08•20•20 |
| Bast | | 8 — Sa•08•01•20 | 18 — Tu•08•11•20 | 28 — Fr•08•21•20 |
| Sobek | | 9 — Su•08•02•20 | 19 — We•08•12•20 | 29 — Sa•08•22•20 |
| Tauret | | 10 — Mo•08•03•20 | 20 — Th•08•13•20 | 30 Scorpio begins — Su•08•23•20 |
| Mut | 1 — Sa•07•25•20 | 11 — Tu•08•04•20 | 21 — Fr•08•14•20 | |
| Amen | 2 — Su•07•26•20 | 12 — We•08•05•20 | 22 — Sa•08•15•20 | |
| Sekhmet | 3 — Mo•07•27•20 | 13 — Th•08•06•20 | 23 — Su•08•16•20 | |
| Ptah | 4 — Tu•07•28•20 | 14 — Fr•08•07•20 | 24 — Mo•08•17•20 | |
| Hapi | 5 — We•07•29•20 | 15 — Sa•08•08•20 | 25 — Tu•08•18•20 | |

## PLATE 22

Paen Aopet
52581

| Ra | Khnum | Bast | Sobek | Tauret | Mut | Amen | Sekhmet | Ptah | Hapi |
|---|---|---|---|---|---|---|---|---|---|
|  |  |  |  |  | Mo•08•24•20 | Tu•08•25•20 | We•08•26•20 | Th•08•27•20 | Fr•08•28•20 |
|  |  |  |  |  | 1 | 2 | 3 | 4 | 5 |
| Sa•08•29•20 | Su•08•30•20 | Mo•08•31•20 | Tu•09•01•20 | We•09•02•20 | Th•09•03•20 | Fr•09•04•20 | Sa•09•05•20 | Su•09•06•20 | Mo•09•07•20 |
| 6 | 7 | 8 | 9 | 10 | 11 | 12 | 13 | 14 | 15 |
| Tu•09•08•20 | We•09•09•20 | Th•09•10•20 | Fr•09•11•20 | Sa•09•12•20 | Su•09•13•20 | Mo•09•14•20 | Tu•09•15•20 | We•09•16•20 | Th•09•17•20 |
| 16 | 17 | 18 | 19 | 20 | 21 | 22 | 23 | 24 | 25 |
| Fr•09•18•20 | Sa•09•19•20 | Su•09•20•20 | Mo•09•21•20 | Tu•09•22•20 |  |  |  |  |  |
| 26 | 27 | 28 | 29 | 30 Death of Osir; *Sp. Crucifixion* of (Pharaoh) |  |  |  |  |  |

## PLATE 23

| Ra | Khnum | Bast | Sobek | Tauret | Mut | Amen | Sekhmet | Ptah | Hapi |
|---|---|---|---|---|---|---|---|---|---|
| 6 | 7 | 8 | 9 | 10 | 1 Divine Birth (Pharaoh)<br>Libra begins | 2 | 3 | 4 | 5 |
| 16<br>Mo•09•28•20 | 17 Nile Begins to Fall<br>Tu•09•29•20 | 18<br>We•09•30•20 | 19<br>Th•10•01•20 | 20<br>Fr•10•02•20 | 11<br>We•09•23•20 | 12<br>Th•09•24•20 | 13<br>Fr•09•25•20 | 14<br>Sa•09•26•20 | 15<br>Su•09•27•20 |
| 26<br>Th•10•08•20 | 27<br>Fr•10•09•20 | 28<br>Sa•10•10•20 | 29<br>Su•10•11•20 | 30<br>Mo•10•12•20 | 21<br>Sa•10•03•20 | 22<br>Su•10•04•20 | 23<br>Mo•10•05•20 | 24<br>Tu•10•06•20 | 25<br>We•10•07•20 |
| Su•10•18•20 | Mo•10•19•20 | Tu•10•20•20 | We•10•21•20 | Th•10•22•20 | Tu•10•13•20 | We•10•14•20 | Th•10•15•20 | Fr•10•16•20 | Sa•10•17•20 |

## PLATE 24

52581

Ka Hera Ka

| Ra | Khnum | Bast | Sobek | Tauret | Mut | Amen | Sekhmet | Ptah | Hapi |
|---|---|---|---|---|---|---|---|---|---|
| | | | | | 1 First day of Akhet; Virgo begins | 2 | 3 | 4 | 5 |
| | | | | | Fr•10•23•20 | Sa•10•24•20 | Su•10•25•20 | Mo•10•26•20 | Tu•10•27•20 |
| 6 | 7 | 8 | 9 | 10 | 11 | 12 | 13 | 14 | 15 |
| We•10•28•20 | Th•10•29•20 | Fr•10•30•20 | Sa•10•31•20 | Su•11•01•20 | Mo•11•02•20 | Tu•11•03•20 | We•11•04•20 | Th•11•05•20 | Fr•11•06•20 |
| 16 | 17 (1) Passion Play and Festival of Osir; 14-day Pilgrimage | 18 (2) | 19 (3) | 20 (4) | 21 (5) | 22 (6) | 23 (7) | 24 (8) | 25 (9) |
| Sa•11•07•20 | Su•11•08•20 | Mo•11•09•20 | Tu•11•10•20 | We•11•11•20 | Th•11•12•20 | Fr•11•13•20 | Sa•11•14•20 | Su•11•15•20 | Mo•11•16•20 |
| 26 (10) | 27 (11) | 28 (12) | 29 (13) | 30 (14) | | | | | |
| Tu•11•17•20 | We•11•18•20 | Th•11•19•20 | Fr•11•20•20 | Sa•11•21•20 | | | | | |

# PLATE 25

52581

| Ra | Khnum | Bast | Sobek | Tauret | Mut | Amen | Sekhmet | Ptah | Hapi |
|---|---|---|---|---|---|---|---|---|---|
|  |  |  |  |  | 1<br>Leo begins | 2 | 3 | 4 | 5 |
| 6 | 7 | 8 | 9 | 10 | 11<br>Su•11•22•20 | 12<br>Mo•11•23•20 | 13<br>Tu•11•24•20 | 14<br>We•11•25•20 | 15<br>Th•11•26•20 |
| 16<br>Fr•11•27•20 | 17<br>Sa•11•28•20 | 18<br>Su•11•29•20 | 19<br>Mo•11•30•20 | 20<br>Tu•12•01•20 | 21<br>We•12•02•20 | 22<br>Th•12•03•20 | 23<br>Fr•12•04•20 | 24<br>Sa•12•05•20 | 25<br>Su•12•06•20 |
| 26 Three-Day Search of Iset<br>Mo•12•07•20 | 27<br>Tu•12•08•20 | 28<br>We•12•09•20 | 29 Spiritual Revival of Osir; Sp. Revival (Pharaoh); Nile Flood Stage Ends<br>Th•12•10•20 | 30 Conception of Heru<br>Fr•12•11•20 | Sa•12•12•20 | Su•12•13•20 | Mo•12•14•20 | Tu•12•15•20 | We•12•16•20 |
| Th•12•17•20 | Fr•12•18•20 | Sa•12•19•20 | Su•12•20•20 | Mo•12•21•20 |  |  |  |  |  |

## PLATE 26

Makhiar — 52581

| Ra | Khnum | Bast | Sobek | Tauret | Mut | Amen | Sekhmet | Ptah | Hapi |
|---|---|---|---|---|---|---|---|---|---|
| | | | | | 1 Tu•12•22•20 — Kheper begins | 2 We•12•23•20 | 3 Th•12•24•20 | 4 Fr•12•25•20 — Birth of Heru (as a newborn babe); *Sp. Rebirth* of (Pharaoh) | 5 Sa•12•26•20 |
| 6 Su•12•27•20 | 7 Mo•12•28•20 | 8 Tu•12•29•20 | 9 We•12•30•20 | 10 Th•12•31•20 | 11 Fr•01•01•21 | 12 Sa•01•02•21 | 13 Su•01•03•21 | 14 Mo•01•04•21 | 15 Tu•01•05•21 |
| 16 We•01•06•21 | 17 Th•01•07•21 | 18 Fr•01•08•21 | 19 Sa•01•09•21 | 20 Su•01•10•21 | 21 Mo•01•11•21 | 22 Tu•01•12•21 | 23 We•01•13•21 | 24 Th•01•14•21 | 25 Fr•01•15•21 |
| 26 Sa•01•16•21 | 27 Su•01•17•21 | 28 Mo•01•18•21 | 29 Tu•01•19•21 | 30 We•01•20•21 — Gemini begins | | | | | |

# PLATE 27

Paen Amenhotep

| | | | | | |
|---|---|---|---|---|---|
| **Ra** | 6 | Tu•01•26•21 | 16 | Fr•02•05•21 | 26 Three-Day Battle: Heru and Seth |
| | Mo•02•15•21 | | | | |
| **Khnum** | 7 | We•01•27•21 | 17 | Sa•02•06•21 | 27 |
| | Tu•02•16•21 | | | | |
| **Bast** | 8 | Th•01•28•21 | 18 | Su•02•07•21 | 28 |
| | We•02•17•21 | | | | |
| **Sobek** | 9 | Fr•01•29•21 | 19 | Mo•02•08•21 | 29 |
| | Th•02•18•21 | | | | |
| **Tauret** | 10 | Sa•01•30•21 | 20 | Tu•02•09•21 | 30 Taurus begins |
| | Fr•02•19•21 | | | | |
| **Mut** | 1 | Th•01•21•21 | 11 | Su•01•31•21 | 21 |
| | We•02•10•21 | | | | |
| **Amen** | 2 | Fr•01•22•21 | 12 | Mo•02•01•21 | 22 |
| | Th•02•11•21 | | | | |
| **Sekhmet** | 3 | Sa•01•23•21 | 13 | Tu•02•02•21 | 23 |
| | Fr•02•12•21 | | | | |
| **Ptah** | 4 | Su•01•24•21 | 14 | We•02•03•21 | 24 |
| | Sa•02•13•21 | | | | |
| **Hapi** | 5 | Mo•01•25•21 | 15 | Th•02•04•21 | 25 |
| | Su•02•14•21 | | | | |

52581

Paen Renfiutet · 52581

| | Ra | Khnum | Bast | Sobek | Tauret | Mut | Amen | Sekhmet | Ptah | Hapi |
|---|---|---|---|---|---|---|---|---|---|---|
| | 6 | 7 | 8 | 9 | 10 | 1 First day of Pert | 2 | 3 | 4 | 5 |
| | Th•02•25•21 16 | Fr•02•26•21 17 | Sa•02•27•21 18 | Su•02•28•21 19 | Mo•03•01•21 20 | Sa•02•20•21 11 | Su•02•21•21 12 | Mo•02•22•21 13 | Tu•02•23•21 14 | We•02•24•21 15 |
| | Su•03•07•21 26 Entombment of Osir; Entombment of (former Pharaoh) | Mo•03•08•21 27 | Tu•03•09•21 28 | We•03•10•21 29 | Th•03•11•21 30 Resurrection of Osir; Resurrection (proper) of former Pharaoh; Aries begins | Tu•03•02•21 21 | We•03•03•21 22 | Th•03•04•21 23 | Fr•03•05•21 24 | Sa•03•06•21 25 |
| | We•03•17•21 | Th•03•18•21 | Fr•03•19•21 | Sa•03•20•21 | Su•03•21•21 | Fr•03•12•21 | Sa•03•13•21 | Su•03•14•21 | Mo•03•15•21 | Tu•03•16•21 |

# PLATE 29

**Paen Khonsu**

| |  | | | | | | |
|---|---|---|---|---|---|---|---|
| | Ra | 6 | Sa•03•27•21 | 16 | Tu•04•06•21 | 26 | Fr•04•16•21 |
| | Khnum | 7 | Su•03•28•21 | 17 | We•04•07•21 | 27 | Sa•04•17•21 |
| | Bast | 8 | Mo•03•29•21 | 18 | Th•04•08•21 | 28 | Su•04•18•21 |
| | Sobek | 9 | Tu•03•30•21 | 19 | Fr•04•09•21 | 29 | Mo•04•19•21 |
| | Tauret | 10 | We•03•31•21 | 20 | Sa•04•10•21 | 30 Pisces begins | Tu•04•20•21 |
| 1 Accession of the new king | Mut | 11 Mo•03•22•21 | Th•04•01•21 | 21 | Su•04•11•21 | | |
| 2 | Amen | 12 Tu•03•23•21 | Fr•04•02•21 | 22 | Mo•04•12•21 | | |
| 3 | Sekhmet | 13 We•03•24•21 | Sa•04•03•21 | 23 | Tu•04•13•21 | | |
| 4 Spiritual Resurrection of the new king | Ptah | 14 Th•03•25•21 | Su•04•04•21 | 24 | We•04•14•21 | | |
| 5 | Hapi | 15 Fr•03•26•21 | Mo•04•05•21 | 25 | Th•04•15•21 | | |

52581

## PLATE 30

52581

Paen Aynit

| Ra | Khnum | Bast | Sobek | Tauret | Mut | Amen | Sekhmet | Ptah | Hapi |
|---|---|---|---|---|---|---|---|---|---|
| | | | | | We•04•21•21 1 | Th•04•22•21 2 | Fr•04•23•21 3 | Sa•04•24•21 4 | Su•04•25•21 5 |
| Mo•04•26•21 6 | Tu•04•27•21 7 | We•04•28•21 8 | Th•04•29•21 9 | Fr•04•30•21 10 | Sa•05•01•21 11 | Su•05•02•21 12 | Mo•05•03•21 13 | Tu•05•04•21 14 | We•05•05•21 15 |
| Th•05•06•21 16 | Fr•05•07•21 17 | Sa•05•08•21 18 | Su•05•09•21 19 | Mo•05•10•21 20 | Tu•05•11•21 21 | We•05•12•21 22 | Th•05•13•21 23 | Fr•05•14•21 24 | Sa•05•15•21 25 |
| Su•05•16•21 26 | Mo•05•17•21 27 | Tu•05•18•21 28 | We•05•19•21 29 | Th•05•20•21 30 | | | | | |

# PLATE 31

| Ra | Khnum | Bast | Sobek | Tauret | Mut | Amen | Sekhmet | Ptah | Hapi |
|---|---|---|---|---|---|---|---|---|---|
|  |  |  |  |  | 1<br>Aquarius begins | 2 | 3 | 4 | 5 |
| 6 | 7 | 8 | 9 | 10 | 11 Disappearance of Sepdta; 70-Day Embalming of _former_ Pharaoh<br>Fr•05•21•21 | 12<br>Sa•05•22•21 | 13<br>Su•05•23•21 | 14<br>Mo•05•24•21 | 15<br>Tu•05•25•21 |
| 16<br>We•05•26•21 | 17<br>Th•05•27•21 | 18<br>Fr•05•28•21 | 19<br>Sa•05•29•21 | 20<br>Su•05•30•21 | 21<br>Mo•05•31•21 | 22<br>Tu•06•01•21 | 23<br>We•06•02•21 | 24<br>Th•06•03•21 | 25<br>Fr•06•04•21 |
| 26<br>Sa•06•05•21 | 27<br>Su•06•06•21 | 28<br>Mo•06•07•21 | 29<br>Tu•06•08•21 | 30<br>We•06•09•21 | Th•06•10•21 | Fr•06•11•21 | Sa•06•12•21 | Su•06•13•21 | Mo•06•14•21 |
| Tu•06•15•21 | We•06•16•21 | Th•06•17•21 | Fr•06•18•21 | Sa•06•19•21 |  |  |  |  |  |

# PLATE 32

52581

Oup Renpet (The Calendrical Five-Day Period)

| Ra | Khnum | Bast | Sobek | Tauret | Mut | Amen | Sekhmet | Ptah | Hapi |
|----|-------|------|-------|--------|-----|------|---------|------|------|
| | | | | | 1 Birthday of Osir; Nile Begins to Rise | 2 Birthday of Heru-ur (*i.e.*, Heru as an Elder) Capricorn begins | 3 Birthday of Seth; "Jurisdiction of the Great Divine Ennead"[1] | 4 Birthday of Iset | 5 Birthday of Nebt-Het |
| | | | | | Su•06•20•21 | Mo•06•21•21 | Tu•06•22•21 | We•06•23•21 | Th•06•24•21 |

1. Maulana Karenga, Maat: The Moral Ideal in Ancient Egypt, (Los Angeles: University of Sankore Press, 2006), 206.

# BIBLIOGRAPHY

Adams, W. Marsham. *Book of the Master: Or the Egyptian Doctrine of the Light Born of the Virgin Mother*. New York: G. P. Putnam's Sons, 1898.

Allen, James P. *Middle Egyptian: An Introduction to the Language and Culture of Hieroglyphs*. New York: Cambridge University Press, 2001.

Allen, James P. *The Ancient Egyptian Pyramid Texts*. Atlanta: Society of Biblical Literature. 2005.

Baedeker Karl. *Egypt: Handbook for Travellers*. Fifth Edition. New York: Charles Scribner's Sons, 1902.

Bakich, Michael E. *The Cambridge Guide to the Constellations*. New York: Cambridge University Press, 1995.

Bakr, A. Abu. "Pharaonic Egypt." In *General History of Africa, II: Ancient Civilizations of Africa*, 84-111. Edited by G. Mokhtar. Berkeley: University of California Press, 1981.

Belmonte, Juan Antonio. "The Egyptian Calendar: Keeping Ma'at on Earth." In *In Search of Cosmic Order: Selected Essays on Egyptian Archaeoastronomy*, 77-131. Edited by Juan Antonio Belmonte and Mosalam Shaltout. Cairo: Supreme Council of Antiquities, 2009.

Best, Susie M. *World Famous Stories in Historic Settings: Egypt and Her Neighbors*. New York: The Macmillan Company, 1918.

Beyerlin, Walter. ed. *Near Eastern Religious Texts Relating to the Old Testament*. Philadelphia: The Westminster Press, 1978.

Blavatsky, H. P. *The Secret Doctrine*. Volume II, Third and Revised Edition. London: The Theosophical Publishing House, 1893.

Bonaparte, Napoleon. *Description De L'Egypte*. Tome 4. Planches. Paris: De L'Imprimerie Royale, 1817.

Bonwick, James. *Egyptian Belief and Modern Thought*, London: C. Kegan Paul & Co., 1878.

Breasted, James Henry. "The Beginnings of Time-Measurement and the Origins of Our Calendar." In *Time and Its Mysteries: Series 1*, 59-94. Washington Square: New York University Press, 1936.

Brier, Bob. *The History of Ancient Egypt: Course Guidebook*. Chantilly: The Great Courses, 1999.

Briggs, Philip. *Ethiopia*. Sixth Edition. Guilford: The Globe Pequot Press Inc., 2012.

Brophy, Thomas G. *The Origin Map: Discovery of a Prehistoric, Megalithic, Astrophysical Map and Sculpture of the Universe*. New York: Writers Club Press, 2002.

Budge, E. A. Wallis. *A History of Egypt*. Volume I. London: Kegan Paul, Trench, Trubner & Co., Ltd., 1902.

Budge, E. A. Wallis. *A History of Egypt*. Volume IV. New York: Oxford University Press, 1902.

Budge, E. A. Wallis. *An Egyptian Hieroglyphic Dictionary: In Two Volumes*. Volume I. London: John Murray, 1920.

Budge, E. A. Wallis. *An Egyptian Hieroglyphic Dictionary: In Two Volumes*. Volume II. London: John Murray, 1920.

Budge, E. A. Wallis. *Egypt*. New York: Henry Holt and Company, 1925.

Budge, E. A. Wallis. *Egyptian Ideas of the Future Life*. Second Edition. London: Kegan Paul, Trench, Trubner & Co., Ltd., 1900.

Budge, E. A. Wallis. *Egyptian Language: Easy Lessons in Egyptian Hieroglyphics*. London: Routledge & Kegan Paul Limited, 1973.

Budge, E. A. Wallis. *Egyptian Magic*. London: Kegan Paul, Trench, Trubner & Co., Ltd., 1901.

Budge, E. A. Wallis. *Facsimiles of Egyptian Hieratic Papyri in the British Museum*. Series 1. London: Oxford University Press, 1910.

Budge, E. A. Wallis. *First Steps in Egyptian: A Book for Beginners*. London: Kegan Paul, Trench, Trubner & Co., Ltd., 1895.

Budge, E. A. Wallis. *From Fetish to God in Ancient Egypt*. New York: Dover Publications, Inc., 1988.

Budge, E. A. Wallis. *Legends of Our Lady Mary the Perpetual Virgin and Her Mother Hanna*. London: The Medici Society, 1922.

Budge, E. A. Wallis. *Legends of the Egyptian Gods: Hieroglyphic Texts and Translations*. New York: Dover Publications, Inc., 1994.

Budge, E. A. Wallis. *Osiris and the Egyptian Resurrection*. Volume I. New York: G. P. Putnam's Sons, 1911.

Budge, E. A. Wallis. *Osiris and the Egyptian Resurrection*. Volume II. New York: G. P. Putnam's Sons, 1911.

Budge, E. A. Wallis. *The Book of Kings*. Volume I, Dynasties I-XIX. London: Kegan Paul, Trench, Trubner & Co., Ltd., 1908.

Budge, E. A. Wallis. *The Book of Kings*. Volume II, Dynasties XX-XXX. London: Kegan Paul, Trench, Trubner & Co., Ltd., 1908.

Budge, E. A. Wallis. *The Book of the Dead: The Papyrus of Ani*. In Two Volumes, Volume II, London: The Medici Society, Ltd., 1913.

Budge, E. A. Wallis. *The Book of the Dead: The Papyrus of Ani in the British Museum*. London: Kegan Paul, Trench, Trubner & Co., 1895.

Budge, E. A. Wallis. *The Gods of the Egyptians: Or, Studies in Egyptian Mythology*. Volume I. London: Methuen & Company, 1904.

Budge, E. A. Wallis *The Gods of the Egyptians: Or, Studies in Egyptian Mythology*. Volume II. London: Methuen & Company, 1904.

Budge, E. A. Wallis. *The Literature of the Ancient Egyptians*. London: J. M. Dent & Sons Limited, 1914.

Budge, E. A. Wallis. *The Mummy: A Handbook of Egyptian Funerary Archaeology*. Second Edition, Revised & Greatly Enlarged. London: Cambridge University Press, 1925.

Budge, E. A. Wallis. Tutankhamen: *Amenism, Atenism and Egyptian Monotheism*. London: Martin Hopkinson, 1923.

Burnham Jr., Robert. *Burnham's Celestial Handbook: An Observer's Guide to the Universe Beyond the Solar System*. Volume I, Revised and Enlarged Edition. Mineola: Dover Publications, Inc., 1978.

Burnham Jr., Robert. *Burnham's Celestial Handbook: An Observer's Guide to the Universe Beyond the Solar System*. Volume II, Revised and Enlarged Edition. Mineola: Dover Publications, Inc., 1978.

Busenbark, Ernest. *Symbols, Sex, and the Stars in Popular Beliefs*. New York: The Truth Seeker Company, Inc., 1949.

CDC. *Pictorial Keys to Arthropods, Reptiles, Birds and Mammals of Public Health Significance*. Atlanta: U.S. Department of Health, Education, and Welfare, 1966.

Cerny, Jaroslav. "The Origin of the Name of the Month Tybi." In *Annales Du Service Des Antiquites De L'Egypte*, Tome XLIII, 173-181. Cairo: Imprimerie De L'Institut Francais D'Archeologie Orientale, 1943.

Chaisson, Eric and Steve McMillan. *Astronomy: A Beginner's Guide to the Universe*. Fifth Edition. Upper Saddle River: Pearson Prentice Hall, 2007.

Chace, Arnold Buffum. *The Rhind Mathematical Papyrus*. Oberlin: Mathematical Association of America, 1979.

Clark, Rosemary. *The Sacred Magic of Ancient Egypt*. St. Paul: Llewellyn Publications, 2003.

Condon, R. J. *Our Pagan Christmas*. Austin: American Atheist Press, 1989.

Coryn, Sidney G. P. *The Faith of Ancient Egypt*. New York: Theosophical Publishing Company, 1913.

Crum, W. E. *A Coptic Dictionary*. New York: Oxford University Press, 1939.

Darby, William J., Paul Ghalioungui and Louis Grivetti. *Food: The Gift of Osiris*. Volume 1. London: Academic Press, 1977.

Denison, Edmund Beckett. *Astronomy Without Mathematics*. New York: G. P. Putnam & Sons, 1869.

Denon, Vivant. *Voyage Dans La Basse Et La Haute Egypte*. Planches. London: M. Peltier, 1802.

Dickerman, Lysander. "The Deities of Ancient Egypt." In *The Andover Review: A Religious and Theological Monthly* 3 (January - June 1885): 374-390.

Diop, Cheikh Anta. *Civilization or Barbarism: An Authentic Anthropology*. Brooklyn: Lawrence Hill Books, 1991.

Diop, Cheikh Anta. "Origin of the Ancient Egyptians." In *Journal of African Civilizations* 4, no. 2 (1982): 9-37.

Diop, Cheikh Anta. *The African Origin of Civilization: Myth or Reality*. Chicago: Lawrence Hill Books, 1974.

Diop, Cheikh Anta. *The Cultural Unity of Black Africa*. London: Karnak House, 1989.

Drummond, Sir W. *The Oedipus Judaicus*. London: A. J. Valpy, Took's Coury, Chancery Lane, 1811.

Elhassan, Ahmed Abuelgasim. *Religious Motifs in Meroitic Painted and Stamped Pottery*. Oxford: John and Erica Hedges Ltd., 2004.

Erman, Adolf. *A Handbook of Egyptian Religion*. London: Archibald Constable & CO. LTD., 1907.

Erman, Adolf. "Monatsnamen aus dem neuen Reich." In *Zeitschrift Fur Agyptische Sprache Und Altertumskunde*, Volume 39, 128-130. Edited by A. Erman and G. Steindorff. Leipzig: J. C. Hinrichs'sche Buchhandlung, 1901.

Erman, Adolf and Hermann Grapow. *Worterbuch Der Aegyptischen Sprache*. Volume 1. Berlin: Akademie -Verlag, 1971.

Fairman, H. W. "Worship and Festivals in an Egyptian Temple." *Bulletin of the John Rylands Library* 37, no. 1 (1954): 165-203.

Gardiner, Alan. *Egyptian Grammar: Being an Introduction to the Study of Hieroglyphs*. Third Edition, Revised. Oxford: Griffith Institute, 1994.

Gardiner, Alan H. "Mesore as First Month of the Egyptian Year." In *Zeitschrift Fur Agyptische Sprache Und Altertumskunde*, Volume 43, 136-144. Edited by A. Erman and G. Steindorff. Leipzig: J. C. Hinrichs'sche Buchhandlung, 1906.

Gardiner, Alan H. "Reviewed Work(s): The Golden Bough: Adonis, Attis, Osiris; Studies in the History of Oriental Religion by J. G. Frazer." *The Journal of Egyptian Archaeology* 2, no. 2 (1915): 121-126.

Goodyear, William Henry. *The Grammar of the Lotus*. London: Sampson Low, Marston & Company, 1891.

Guirand, Felix. *Larousse Encyclopedia of Mythology*. New York: Prometheus Press, 1960.

Hawass, Zahi and Sandro Vannini. *The Lost Tombs of Thebes: Life in Paradise*. London: Thames & Hudson, 2009.

Higgins, Godfrey. *Anacalypsis*. Volume II. London: Longman, Rees, Orme, Brown, Green, and Longman Paternoster Row, 1836.

Hilliard, Asa G. *The Maroon Within Us: Selected Essays on African American Community Socialization*.

Baltimore: Black Classic Press, 1995.

Hornung, Erik, Rolf Krauss and David A. Warburton. *Ancient Egyptian Chronology*. Leiden: Brill, 2006.

James, George G. M. *Stolen Legacy*. Trenton: African World Press, 1992.

Johnston, James. "Traces of a Sabbath in Heathen Lands." In *The Catholic Presbyterian*, Volume V, 179-206. Edited by W. G. Blaikie. New York: A. D. F. Randolph & Co., 1881.

Jones, Rekhety Wimby. "The Calendar Project." In *African World History Project: The Preliminary Challenge*, 103-123. Edited by Jacob H. Carruthers and Leon C. Harris. Los Angeles: Association for the Study of Classical African Civilizations, 1997.

Karenga, Maulana. *Introduction to Black Studies*. Second Edition. Los Angeles: University of Sankore Press, 1993.

Karenga, Maulana. *Kwanzaa & the Dialog with African Culture: Recovery and Reaffirmation* [Audio Presentation]. Us Organization, 1995.

Karenga, Maulana. *Maat: The Moral Ideal in Ancient Egypt*. Los Angeles: University of Sankore Press, 2006.

Karenga, Maulana. *Selections from the Husia*. Los Angeles: University Of Sankore Press, 1984.

Karenga, Maulana. *The Book of Coming Forth by Day: The Ethics of the Declarations of Innocence*. Los Angeles: University of Sankore Press, 1990.

Karenga, Tarík. *Review of the Kemetan Mystery System*. First Edition. Union City: Amenism, Inc., In Press.

Karenga, Tarík. *The Pharaohs' 5 Laws of Success*. First Edition. Union City: Amenism, Inc., 2022.

Kees, Hermann. *Ancient Egypt: A Cultural Topography*. London: Faber and Faber, 1961.

Kwok, Sun. *Our Place in the Universe: Understanding Fundamental Astronomy from Ancient Discoveries*. Second Edition. Cham: Springer International Publishing AG, 2017.

Laertius, Diogenes. *The Lives and Opinions of Eminent Philosophers*. Translated by C. D. Yonge. London: George Bell and Sons, 1901.

Lichtheim, Miriam. *Ancient Egyptian Literature*. Volume I. Los Angeles: University of California Press, 1975.

# Bibliography

Lockyer, Norman. *The Dawn of Astronomy: A Study of the Temple-Worship and Mythology of the Ancient Egyptians.* London: Cassell and Company Limited, 1894.

Mariette-Bey, Auguste. *Monuments Divers Recueillis en Egypte et en Nubie.* Paris: Librairie A. Franck, 1872.

Massey, Gerald. *Ancient Egypt: The Light of the World.* Volume I. London: T. Fisher Unwin, 1907.

Massey, Gerald. *Ancient Egypt: The Light of the World.* Volume II. London: T. Fisher Unwin, 1907.

McKinney-Johnson, Eloise. "Egypt's Isis: The Original Black Madonna." In *Black Women in Antiquity*, 64-71. Edited by Ivan Van Sertima. New Brunswick: Transaction Publishers, 1988.

Mitchell, Logan. *Religion in the Heavens; Or, Mythology Unveiled.* London: Freethought Publishing Company, 1881.

Moncrieff, Colonel Sir Scott. "Engineering." In *Nature* 72, no. 1871, 465-471. Edited by Sir Norman Lockyer. London: MacMillan and Co., Limited, 1905.

Murdock, D. M. *Christ in Egypt: The Horus-Jesus Connection.* Seattle: Stellar House Publishing, 2009.

Mure, William. *A Dissertation on the Calendar and Zodiac of Ancient Egypt.* London: Bell & Bradfute, 1832.

Murphy, Edwin. *The Antiquities of Egypt: A Translation with Notes of Book I of the Library of History of Diodorus Siculus.* New Brunswick: Transaction Publishers, 1990.

Naville, Edouard. "The Litany of Ra." In *Records of the Past*, Volume VIII, Egyptian Texts, 103-128. Edited by Samuel Birch. London: Samuel Bagster and Sons, 1874.

Nordgren, Tyler. *Stars Above, Earth Below: A Guide to Astronomy in the National Parks.* Chichester: Praxis Publishing Ltd., 2010.

Orlin, Eric. ed. *The Routledge Encyclopedia of Ancient Mediterranean Religions.* New York: Routledge, 2016.

Pasachoff, Jay M. Astronomy: *From the Earth to the Universe*, Third Edition. New York: Saunders College Publishing, 1987.

Rawlinson, George. *History of Herodotus.* In Four Volumes. Volume 1, London: John Murray, 1862.

Rawlinson, George. *History of Herodotus.* In Four Volumes. Volume II, London: John Murray, 1862.

Remler, Pat. *Egyptian Mythology A to Z*. Third Edition, New York: Chelsea House Publishers, 2010.

Renouf, P. Le Page. "Inscription of Queen Hatasu on the Base of the Great Obelisk of Karnak," In *Records of the Past*, Volume XII, Egyptian Texts,127-136. Edited by Samuel Birch. London: Samuel Bagster and Sons, 1874.

Renouf, Sir P. Le Page and Prof. E. Naville. *The Egyptian Book of the Dead: Translation and Commentary*. London: The Society of Biblical Archaeology, 1904.

Rhead, G. Woolliscroft. The *Principles of Design*. London: B. T. Batsford, 1905.

Roeder, Gunther. *Short Egyptian Grammar*. New Haven: Yale University Press, 1920.

Rosellini, Ippolito. *I Monumenti Dell' Egitto e Della Nubia*. Tomo Terzo, Monumenti Del Culto. Pisa: Presso Niccolo Capurro, 1844.

Said, Rushdi. *The River Nile: Geology, Hydrology and Utilization*. Tarrytown: Pergamon Press, 1993.

Sakoian, Frances and Louis S. Acker. *The Astrologer's Handbook*. New York: Collins Reference, 1973.

Sauneron, Serge and Jean Yoyotte. "La Naissance Du Monde Selon L'Egypte Ancienne." In *Sources Orientales I: La Naissance Du Monde*, 17-91. Edited by Anne-Marie Esnoul, Paul Garelli, Yves Hervouet, Marcel Leibovici, Serge Sauneron and Jean Yoyotte. Paris: Editions Du Seuil, 1959.

Sayce, A. H. *The Religion of Ancient Egypt and Babylonia*. Edinburgh: T. & T. Clark, 1902.

St. Clair, George. *Creation Records Discovered in Egypt: Studies in the Book of the Dead*. London: David Nutt, 1898.

Starder. *Hand Drawn Corn Vector Design 01* [Digital File]. Retrieved on 11/03/2020 from https://freedesignfile.com/153944-hand-drawn-corn-vector-design-01/.

Stern, Sacha. *Calendars in Antiquity: Empires, States, and Societies*. Oxford: Oxford University Press, 2012.

Tetteh, Benjamin. "2019: Year of Return for African Diaspora." *African Renewal: Dec. 2018 – Mar. 2019*. https://www.un.org/africarenewal/magazine/december-2018-march-2019/2019-year-return-african-diaspora. Accessed 8 October 2020.

The Holy Bible: *Comprising the Old and New Testaments*. The King James Version. New York: American Bible Society, 1972.

Van De Mieroop, Marc. *A History of Ancient Egypt*. Malden: Wiley-Blackwell, 2011.

# Bibliography

Waddell, W. G. *Manetho*. Cambridge: Harvard University Press, 1964.

Warmington, E. H. *Dio's Roman History*. In Nine Volumes. III, Cambridge: Harvard University Press, 1969.

Webster's New World Dictionary & Thesaurus. Version 2.0, Build #25. Accent Software International. Macmillan Publishers, 1998.

Weill, Raymond. *Etudes D'Egyptologie: Bases, Methodes et Resultats de la Chronologie Egyptienne*. Paris: Paul Geuthner, 1926.

White, J. E. Manchip. *Ancient Egypt: Its Culture and History*. New York: Dover Publications Inc., 1970.

Wilkinson, Sir J. Gardner. *The Manners and Customs of the Ancient Egyptians*. Volume II. London: John Murray, 1878.

Wimby, Rekhety. "The Unity of African Languages." In *Kemet and the African Worldview*, 151-166. Edited by Maulana Karenga and Jacob Carruthers. Los Angeles: University of Sankore Press, 1986.

# INDEX

# Index

www.ingramcontent.com/pod-product-compliance
Lightning Source LLC
Chambersburg PA
CBHW062001090426
42811CB00006B/1005